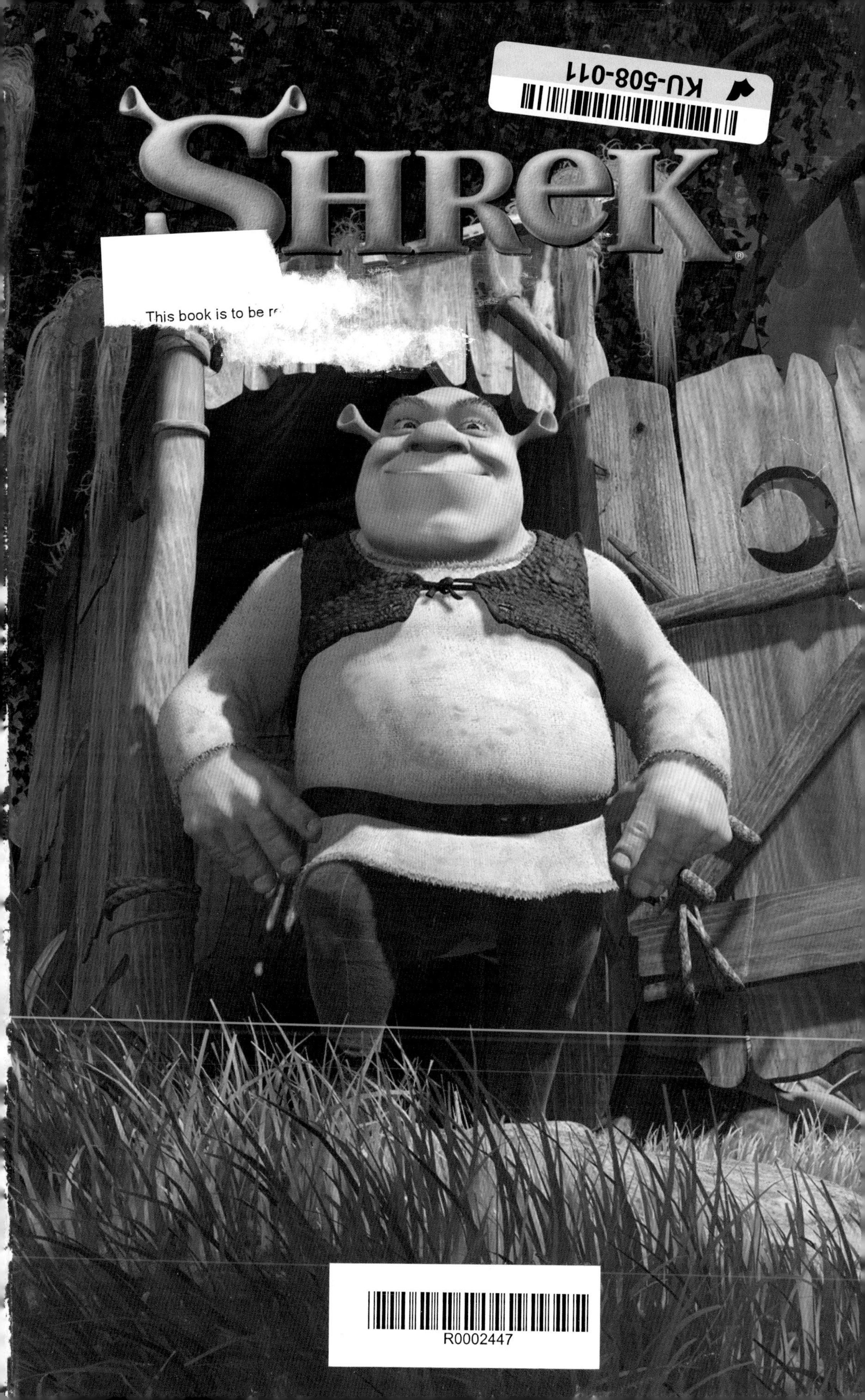
Shrek®

WARRINGTON COLLEGE
LIBRARY

GN

R00024477

9/3/05

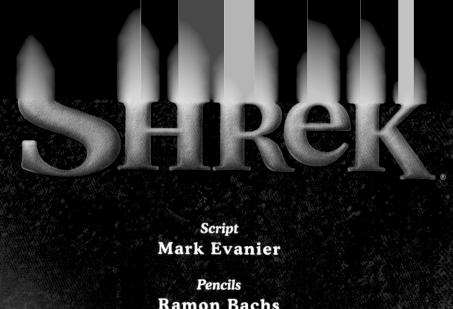

SHReK

Script
Mark Evanier

Pencils
Ramon Bachs

Inks
Raul Fernandez

Colors
Sno Cone

Letters
**Sno Cone and
Virtual Calligraphy's Dave Sharpe**

DreamWorks

Publisher
Mike Richardson

Editor
Dave Land

Editorial Assistant
Katie Moody

Collection Designer
Debra Bailey

SHREK
TM & © 2003 DreamWorks. All rights reserved. No portion of this book may be reproduced or
transmitted in any form or by any means without the express written permission of the publisher.
Names, characters, places and incidents featured in this publication are either the product of the
author's imagination or used fictitiously. Any resemblance to actual persons, living or dead
(except for satirical purposes), is entirely coincidental. A CIP catalogue record for this title is
available from the British Library.

Published by
Titan Books
144 Southwark Street
London
SE1 0UP

First edition: June 2004
ISBN: 1-84023-677-9

13 5 7 9 10 8 6 4 2

Printed in Italy

What did you think of this book? We love to hear from our readers.
Please email us at : readerfeedback@titanemail.com, or write to us at
the above address. You can also visit us at www.titanbooks.com

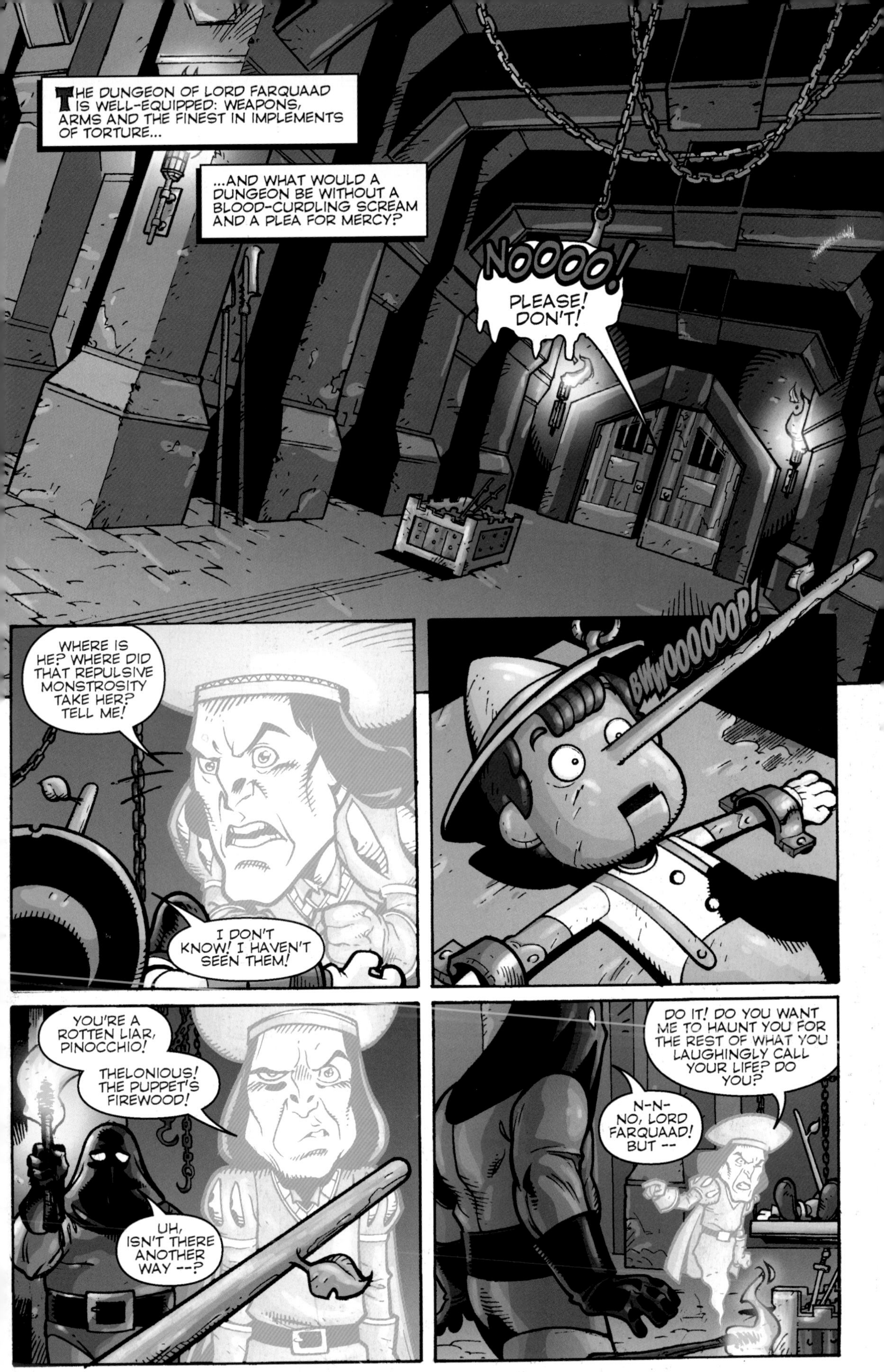
THE DUNGEON OF LORD FARQUAAD IS WELL-EQUIPPED: WEAPONS, ARMS AND THE FINEST IN IMPLEMENTS OF TORTURE...
...AND WHAT WOULD A DUNGEON BE WITHOUT A BLOOD-CURDLING SCREAM AND A PLEA FOR MERCY?
NOOOO! PLEASE! DON'T!
WHERE IS HE? WHERE DID THAT REPULSIVE MONSTROSITY TAKE HER? TELL ME!
I DON'T KNOW! I HAVEN'T SEEN THEM!
BWWOOOOOOP!
YOU'RE A ROTTEN LIAR, PINOCCHIO!
THELONIOUS! THE PUPPET'S FIREWOOD!
UH, ISN'T THERE ANOTHER WAY --?
DO IT! DO YOU WANT ME TO HAUNT YOU FOR THE REST OF WHAT YOU LAUGHINGLY CALL YOUR LIFE? DO YOU?
N-N-NO, LORD FARQUAAD! BUT --

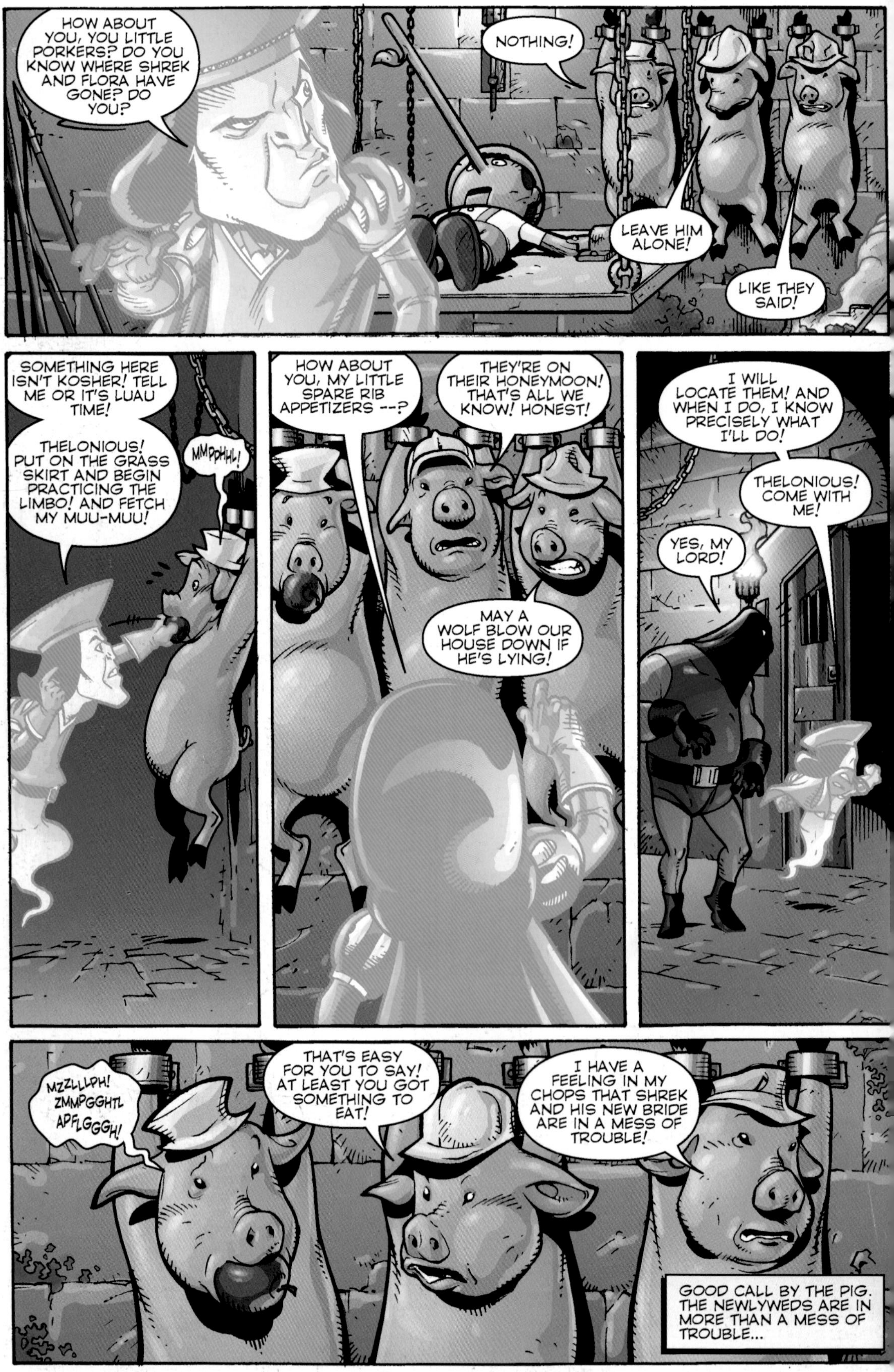
HOW ABOUT YOU, YOU LITTLE PORKERS? DO YOU KNOW WHERE SHREK AND FLORA HAVE GONE? DO YOU?
NOTHING!
LEAVE HIM ALONE!
LIKE THEY SAID!
SOMETHING HERE ISN'T KOSHER! TELL ME OR IT'S LUAU TIME!
THELONIOUS! PUT ON THE GRASS SKIRT AND BEGIN PRACTICING THE LIMBO! AND FETCH MY MUU-MUU!
MMPPHHL!
HOW ABOUT YOU, MY LITTLE SPARE RIB APPETIZERS --?
THEY'RE ON THEIR HONEYMOON! THAT'S ALL WE KNOW! HONEST!
MAY A WOLF BLOW OUR HOUSE DOWN IF HE'S LYING!
I WILL LOCATE THEM! AND WHEN I DO, I KNOW PRECISELY WHAT I'LL DO!
THELONIOUS! COME WITH ME!
YES, MY LORD!
MZZLLLPH! ZMMPGGHTL APFLGGGH!
THAT'S EASY FOR YOU TO SAY! AT LEAST YOU GOT SOMETHING TO EAT!
I HAVE A FEELING IN MY CHOPS THAT SHREK AND HIS NEW BRIDE ARE IN A MESS OF TROUBLE!
GOOD CALL BY THE PIG. THE NEWLYWEDS ARE IN MORE THAN A MESS OF TROUBLE...

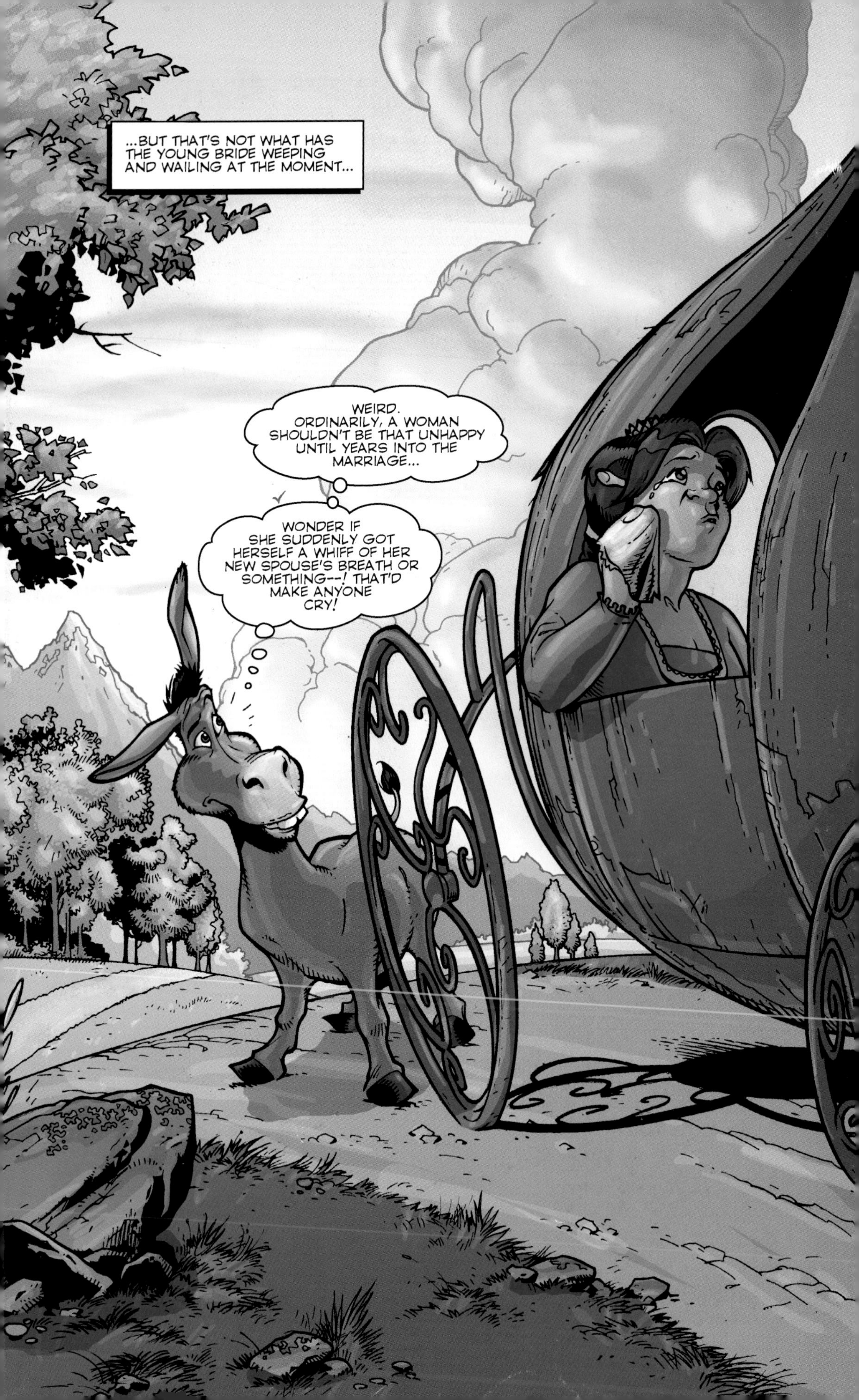
...BUT THAT'S NOT WHAT HAS THE YOUNG BRIDE WEEPING AND WAILING AT THE MOMENT...
WEIRD. ORDINARILY, A WOMAN SHOULDN'T BE THAT UNHAPPY UNTIL YEARS INTO THE MARRIAGE...
WONDER IF SHE SUDDENLY GOT HERSELF A WHIFF OF HER NEW SPOUSE'S BREATH OR SOMETHING--! THAT'D MAKE ANYONE CRY!

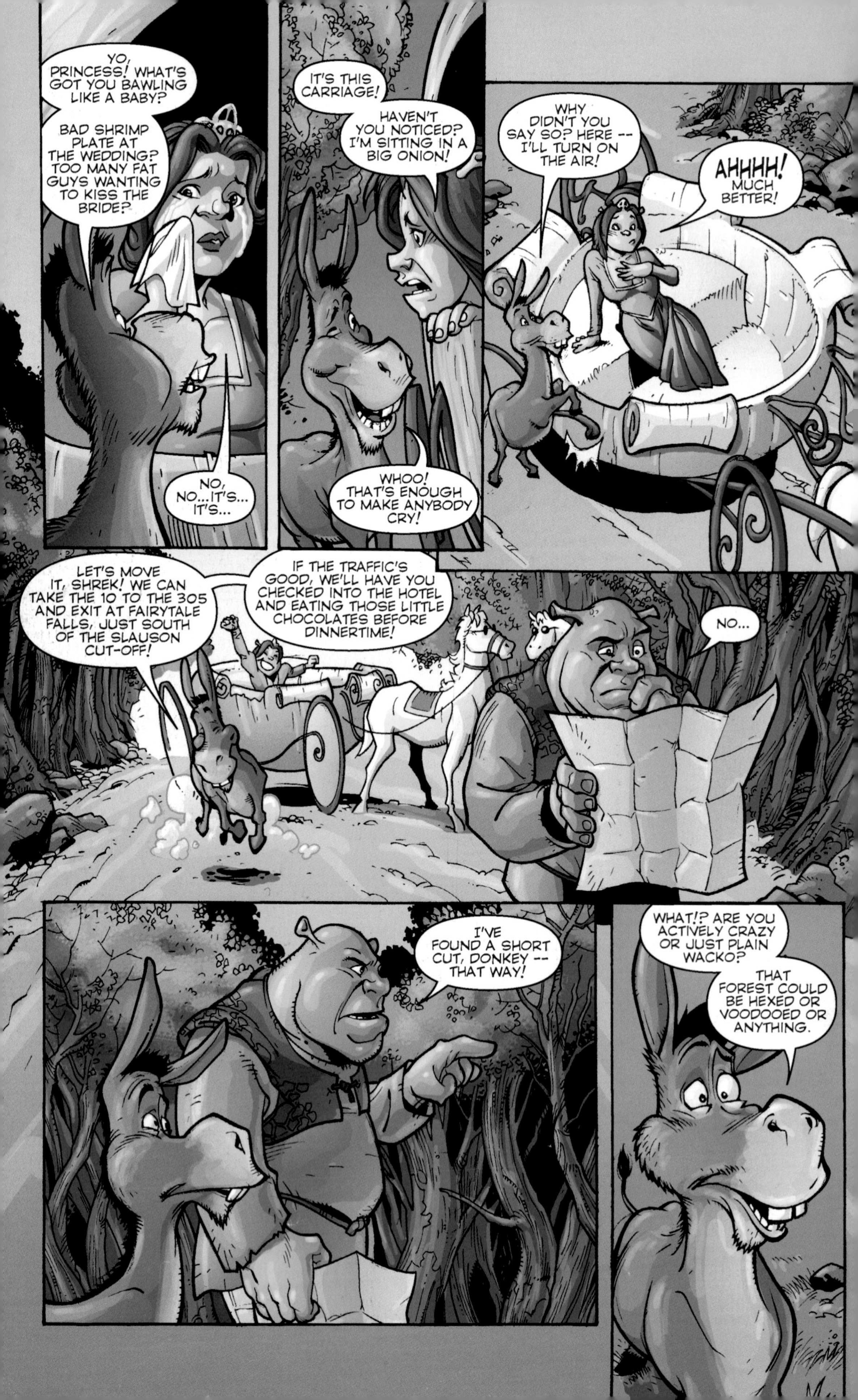
YO, PRINCESS! WHAT'S GOT YOU BAWLING LIKE A BABY?
BAD SHRIMP PLATE AT THE WEDDING? TOO MANY FAT GUYS WANTING TO KISS THE BRIDE?
NO, NO...IT'S... IT'S...
IT'S THIS CARRIAGE!
HAVEN'T YOU NOTICED? I'M SITTING IN A BIG ONION!
WHOO! THAT'S ENOUGH TO MAKE ANYBODY CRY!
WHY DIDN'T YOU SAY SO? HERE -- I'LL TURN ON THE AIR!
AHHHH! MUCH BETTER!
LET'S MOVE IT, SHREK! WE CAN TAKE THE 10 TO THE 305 AND EXIT AT FAIRYTALE FALLS, JUST SOUTH OF THE SLAUSON CUT-OFF!
IF THE TRAFFIC'S GOOD, WE'LL HAVE YOU CHECKED INTO THE HOTEL AND EATING THOSE LITTLE CHOCOLATES BEFORE DINNERTIME!
NO...
I'VE FOUND A SHORT CUT, DONKEY -- THAT WAY!
WHAT!? ARE YOU ACTIVELY CRAZY OR JUST PLAIN WACKO?
THAT FOREST COULD BE HEXED OR VOODOOED OR ANYTHING.

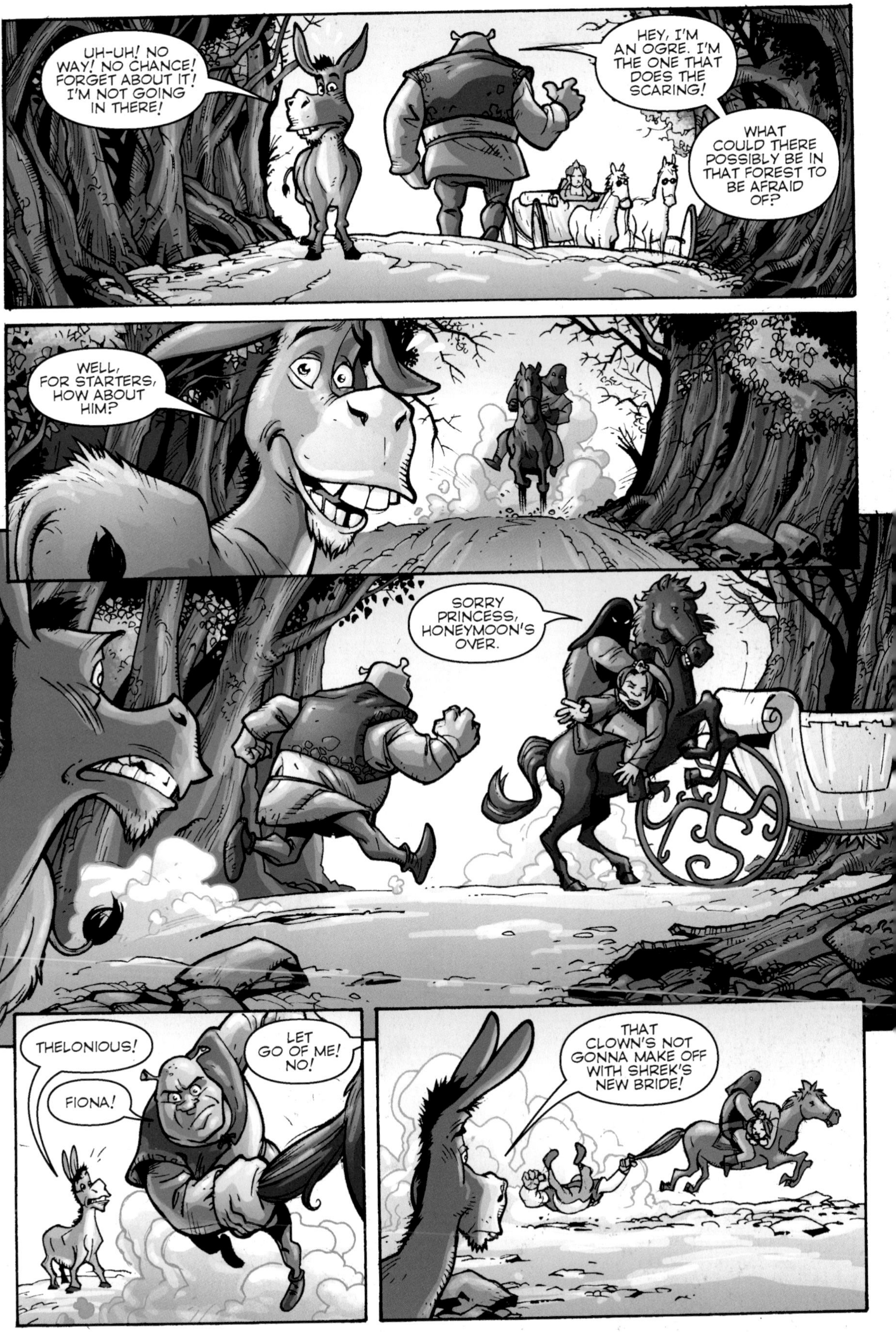
UH-UH! NO WAY! NO CHANCE! FORGET ABOUT IT! I'M NOT GOING IN THERE!
HEY, I'M AN OGRE. I'M THE ONE THAT DOES THE SCARING!
WHAT COULD THERE POSSIBLY BE IN THAT FOREST TO BE AFRAID OF?
WELL, FOR STARTERS, HOW ABOUT HIM?
SORRY PRINCESS, HONEYMOON'S OVER.
THELONIOUS!
LET GO OF ME! NO!
FIONA!
THAT CLOWN'S NOT GONNA MAKE OFF WITH SHREK'S NEW BRIDE!

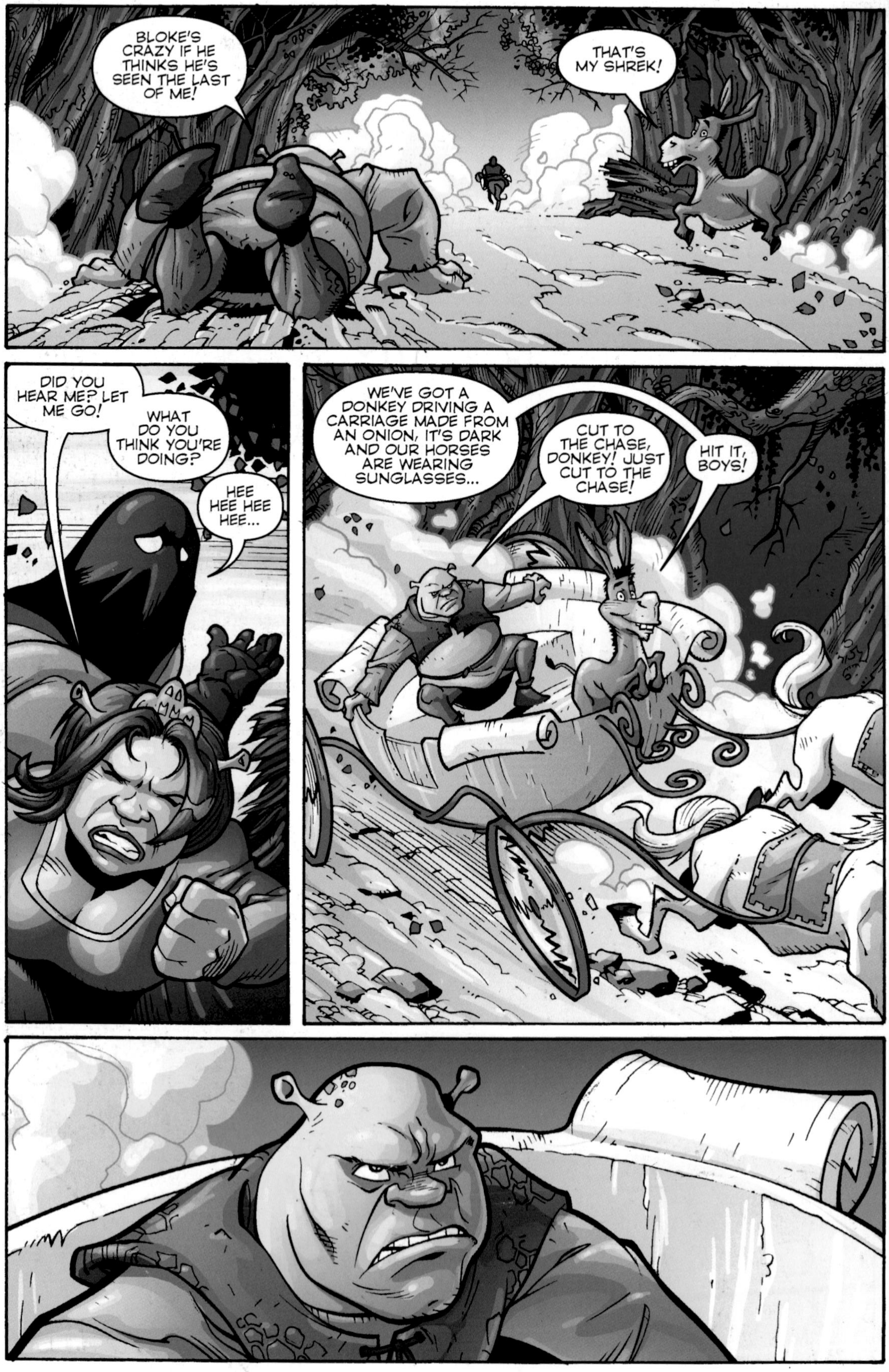
BLOKE'S CRAZY IF HE THINKS HE'S SEEN THE LAST OF ME!
THAT'S MY SHREK!
DID YOU HEAR ME? LET ME GO!
WHAT DO YOU THINK YOU'RE DOING?
HEE HEE HEE HEE...
WE'VE GOT A DONKEY DRIVING A CARRIAGE MADE FROM AN ONION, IT'S DARK AND OUR HORSES ARE WEARING SUNGLASSES...
CUT TO THE CHASE, DONKEY! JUST CUT TO THE CHASE!
HIT IT, BOYS!

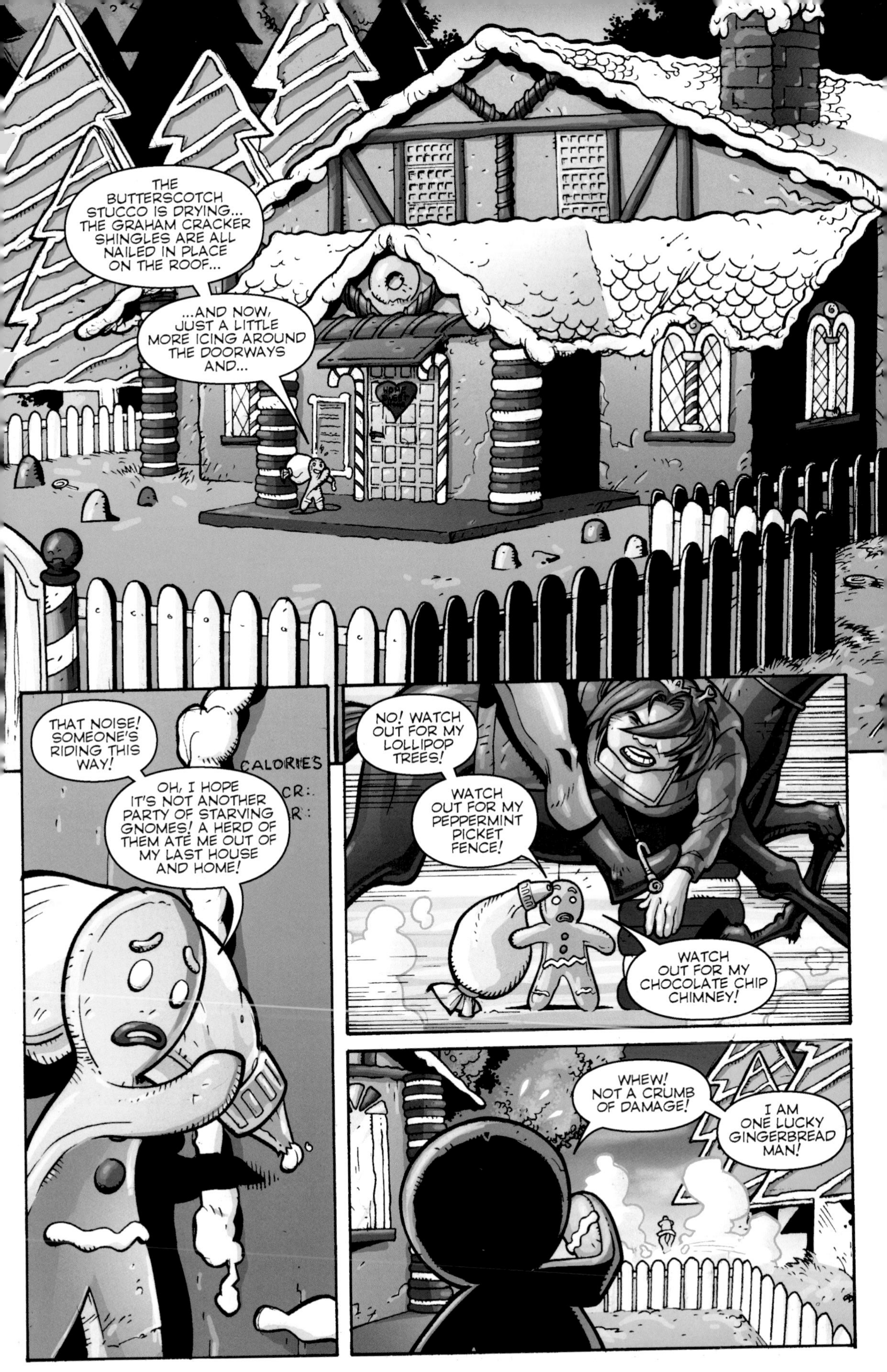
THE BUTTERSCOTCH STUCCO IS DRYING... THE GRAHAM CRACKER SHINGLES ARE ALL NAILED IN PLACE ON THE ROOF...
...AND NOW, JUST A LITTLE MORE ICING AROUND THE DOORWAYS AND...
THAT NOISE! SOMEONE'S RIDING THIS WAY!
CALORIES
OH, I HOPE IT'S NOT ANOTHER PARTY OF STARVING GNOMES! A HERD OF THEM ATE ME OUT OF MY LAST HOUSE AND HOME!
NO! WATCH OUT FOR MY LOLLIPOP TREES!
WATCH OUT FOR MY PEPPERMINT PICKET FENCE!
WATCH OUT FOR MY CHOCOLATE CHIP CHIMNEY!
WHEW! NOT A CRUMB OF DAMAGE!
I AM ONE LUCKY GINGERBREAD MAN!

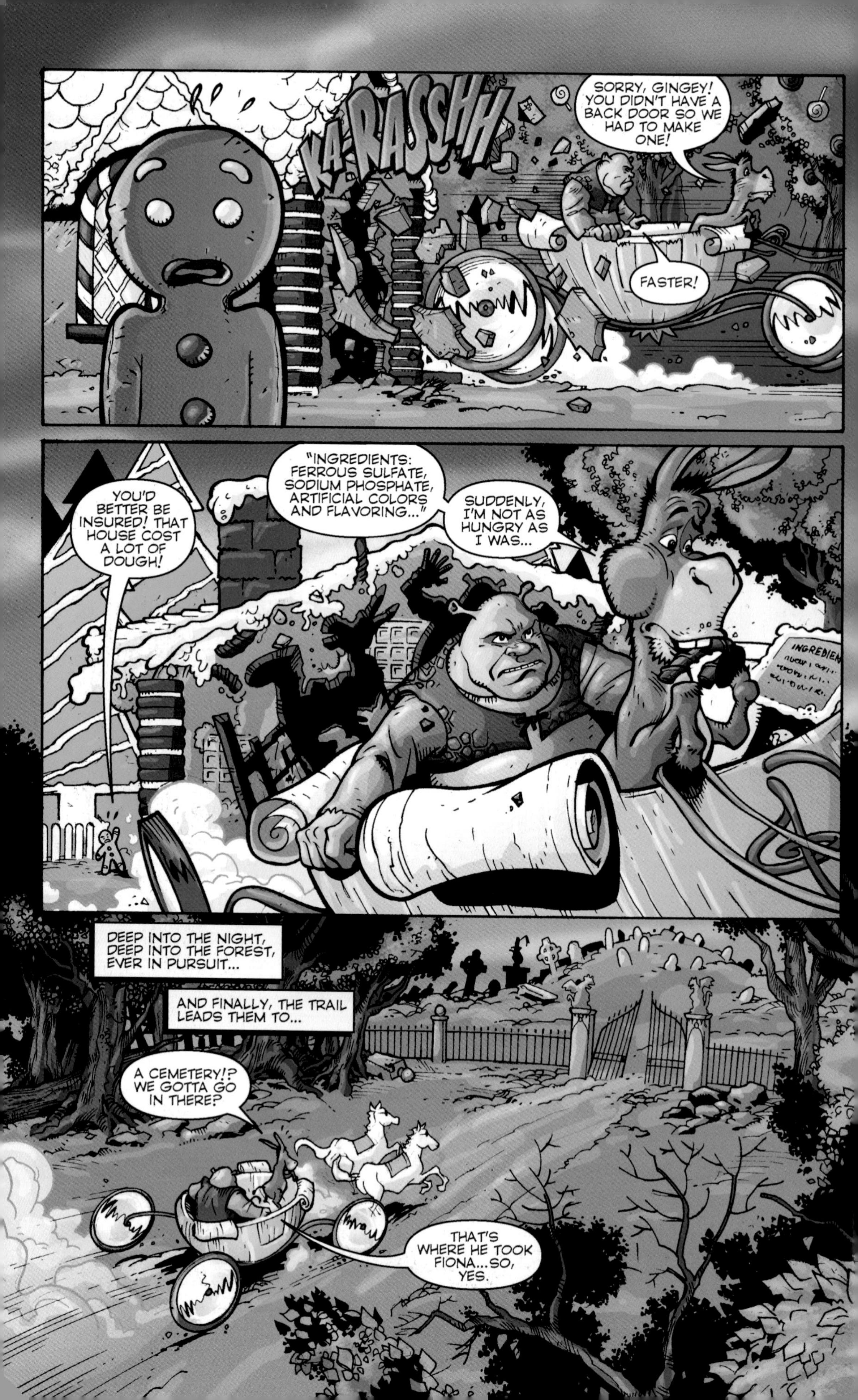
KA-RASSHH
SORRY, GINGEY! YOU DIDN'T HAVE A BACK DOOR SO WE HAD TO MAKE ONE!
FASTER!
YOU'D BETTER BE INSURED! THAT HOUSE COST A LOT OF DOUGH!
"INGREDIENTS: FERROUS SULFATE, SODIUM PHOSPHATE, ARTIFICIAL COLORS AND FLAVORING..."
SUDDENLY, I'M NOT AS HUNGRY AS I WAS...
DEEP INTO THE NIGHT, DEEP INTO THE FOREST, EVER IN PURSUIT...
AND FINALLY, THE TRAIL LEADS THEM TO...
A CEMETERY!? WE GOTTA GO IN THERE?
THAT'S WHERE HE TOOK FIONA... SO, YES.

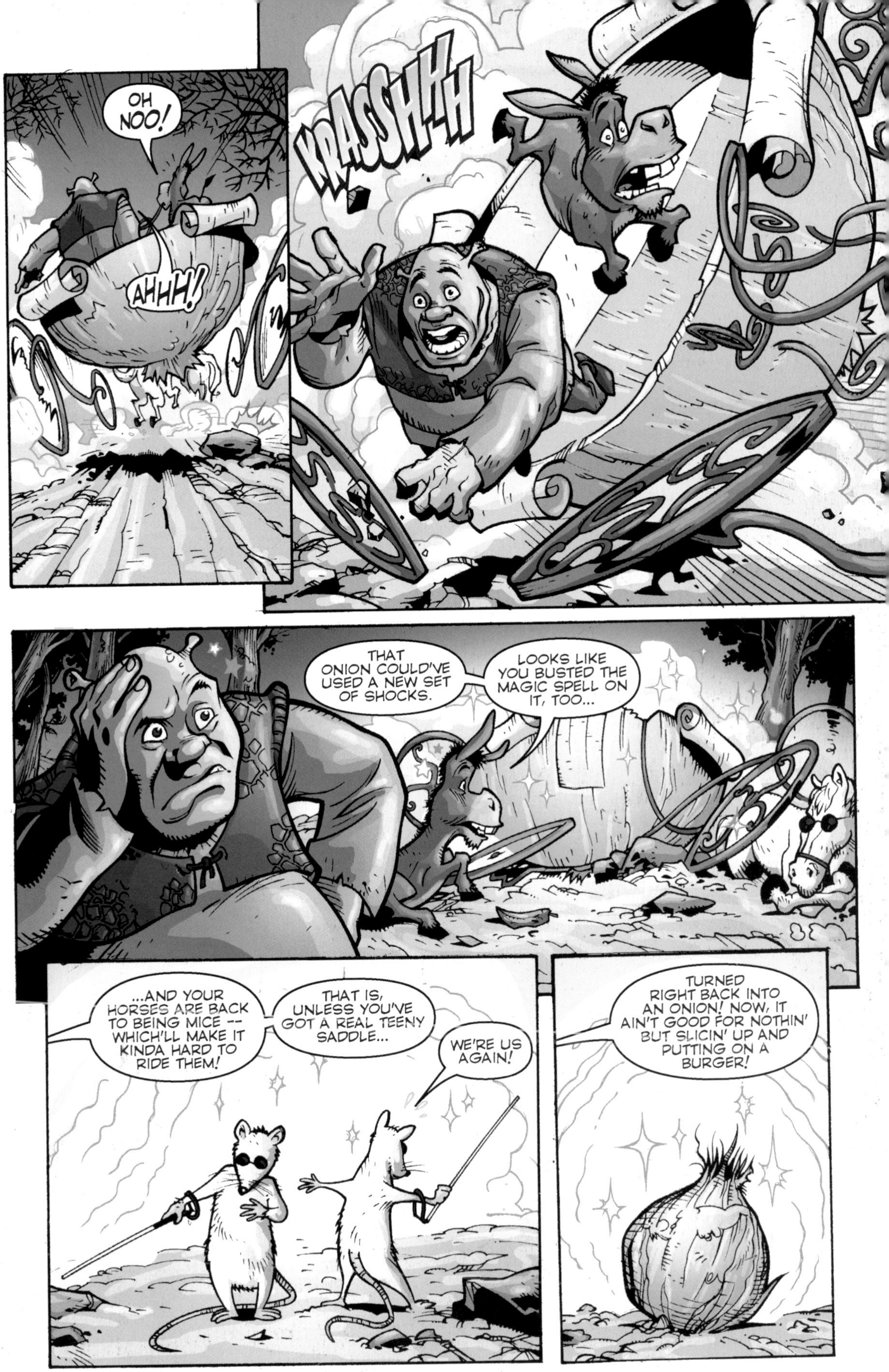
OH NOO!
AHHH!
KRASSHHHH
THAT ONION COULD'VE USED A NEW SET OF SHOCKS.
LOOKS LIKE YOU BUSTED THE MAGIC SPELL ON IT, TOO...
...AND YOUR HORSES ARE BACK TO BEING MICE -- WHICH'LL MAKE IT KINDA HARD TO RIDE THEM!
THAT IS, UNLESS YOU'VE GOT A REAL TEENY SADDLE...
WE'RE US AGAIN!
TURNED RIGHT BACK INTO AN ONION! NOW, IT AIN'T GOOD FOR NOTHIN' BUT SLICIN' UP AND PUTTING ON A BURGER!

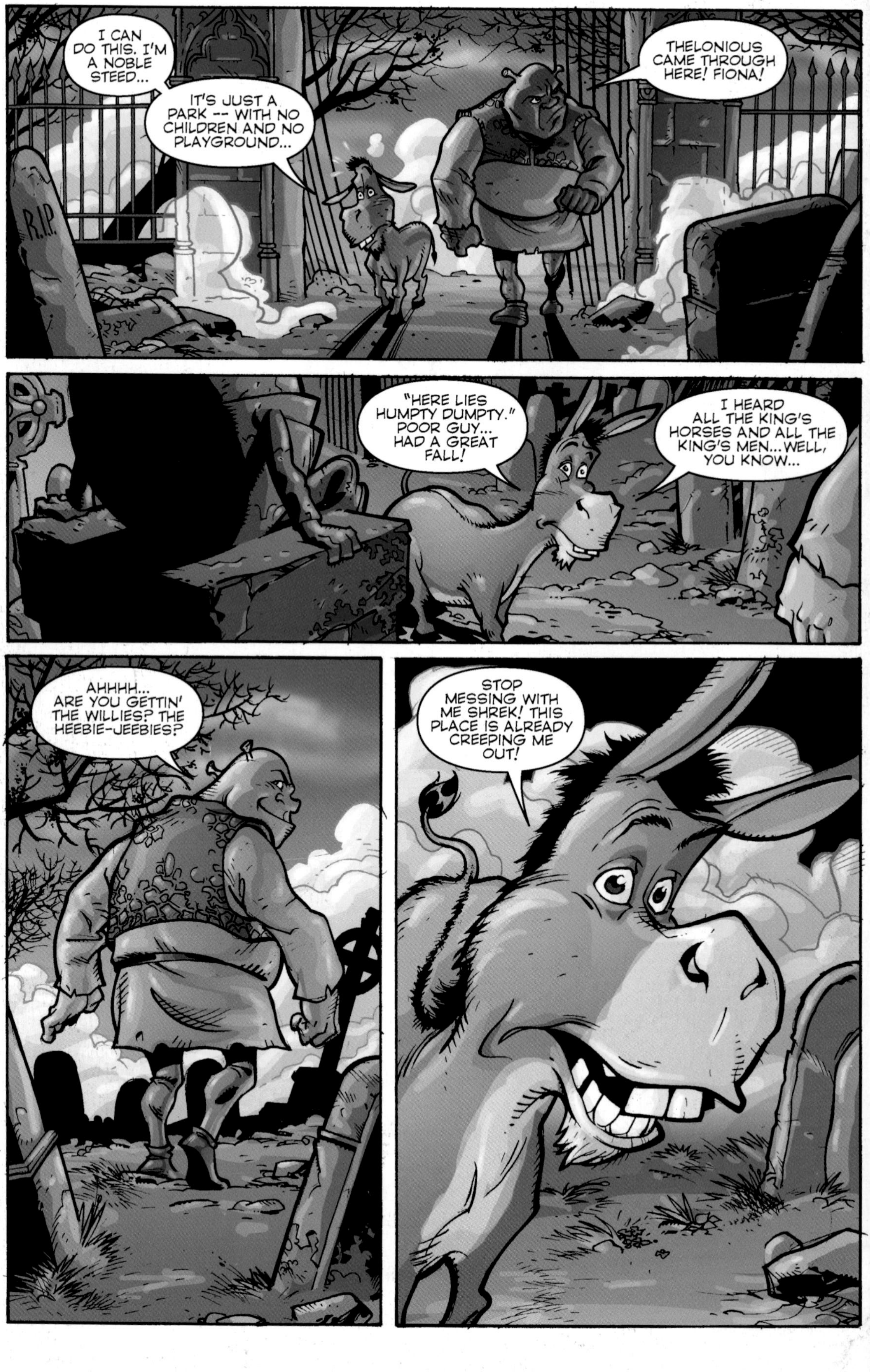
I CAN DO THIS. I'M A NOBLE STEED...
IT'S JUST A PARK -- WITH NO CHILDREN AND NO PLAYGROUND...
THELONIOUS CAME THROUGH HERE! FIONA!
R.I.P.
"HERE LIES HUMPTY DUMPTY." POOR GUY... HAD A GREAT FALL!
I HEARD ALL THE KING'S HORSES AND ALL THE KING'S MEN...WELL, YOU KNOW...
AHHHH... ARE YOU GETTIN' THE WILLIES? THE HEEBIE-JEEBIES?
STOP MESSING WITH ME SHREK! THIS PLACE IS ALREADY CREEPING ME OUT!

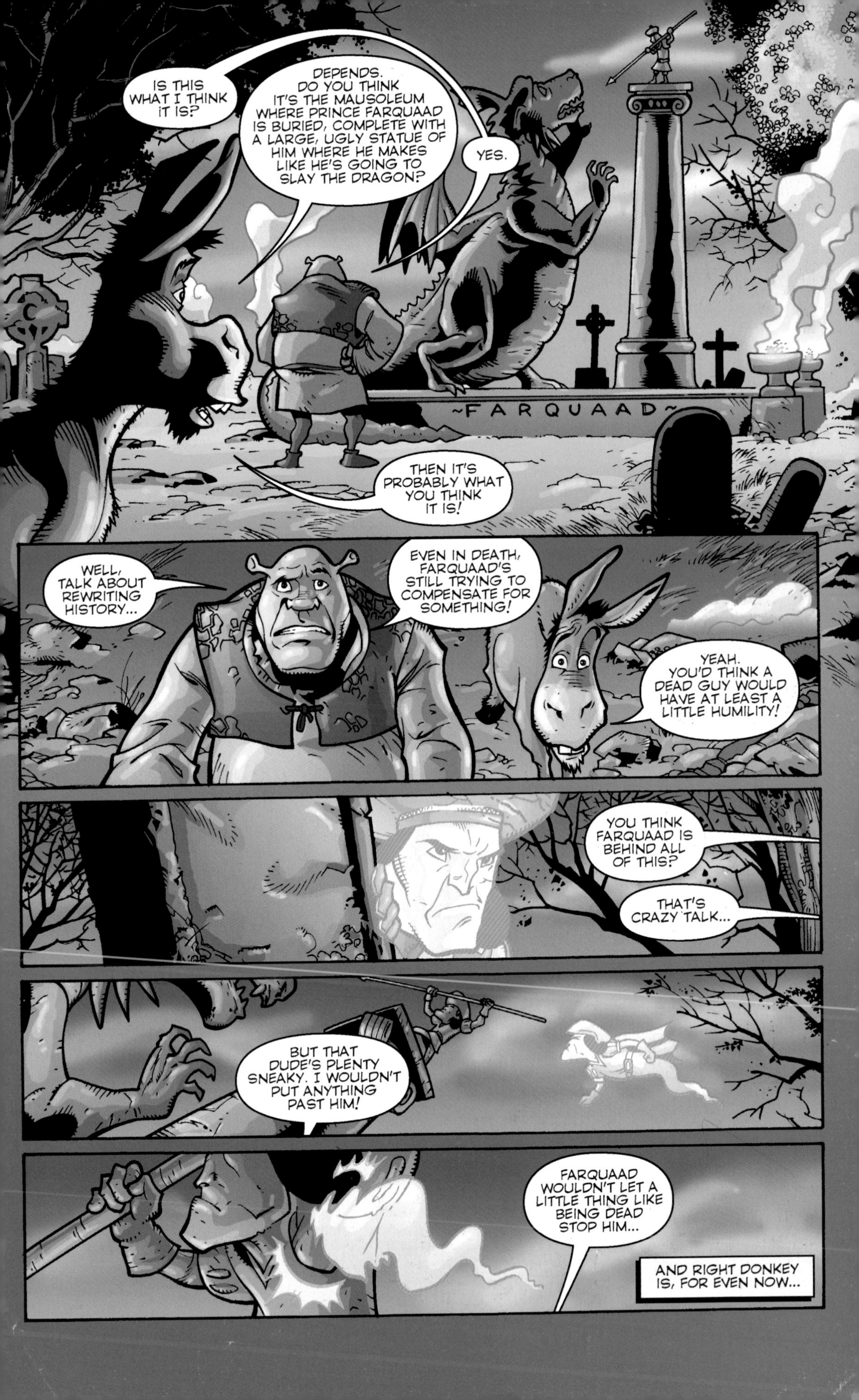
IS THIS WHAT I THINK IT IS?
DEPENDS. DO YOU THINK IT'S THE MAUSOLEUM WHERE PRINCE FARQUAAD IS BURIED, COMPLETE WITH A LARGE, UGLY STATUE OF HIM WHERE HE MAKES LIKE HE'S GOING TO SLAY THE DRAGON?
YES.
THEN IT'S PROBABLY WHAT YOU THINK IT IS!
~FARQUAAD~
WELL, TALK ABOUT REWRITING HISTORY...
EVEN IN DEATH, FARQUAAD'S STILL TRYING TO COMPENSATE FOR SOMETHING!
YEAH. YOU'D THINK A DEAD GUY WOULD HAVE AT LEAST A LITTLE HUMILITY!
YOU THINK FARQUAAD IS BEHIND ALL OF THIS?
THAT'S CRAZY TALK...
BUT THAT DUDE'S PLENTY SNEAKY. I WOULDN'T PUT ANYTHING PAST HIM!
FARQUAAD WOULDN'T LET A LITTLE THING LIKE BEING DEAD STOP HIM...
AND RIGHT DONKEY IS, FOR EVEN NOW...

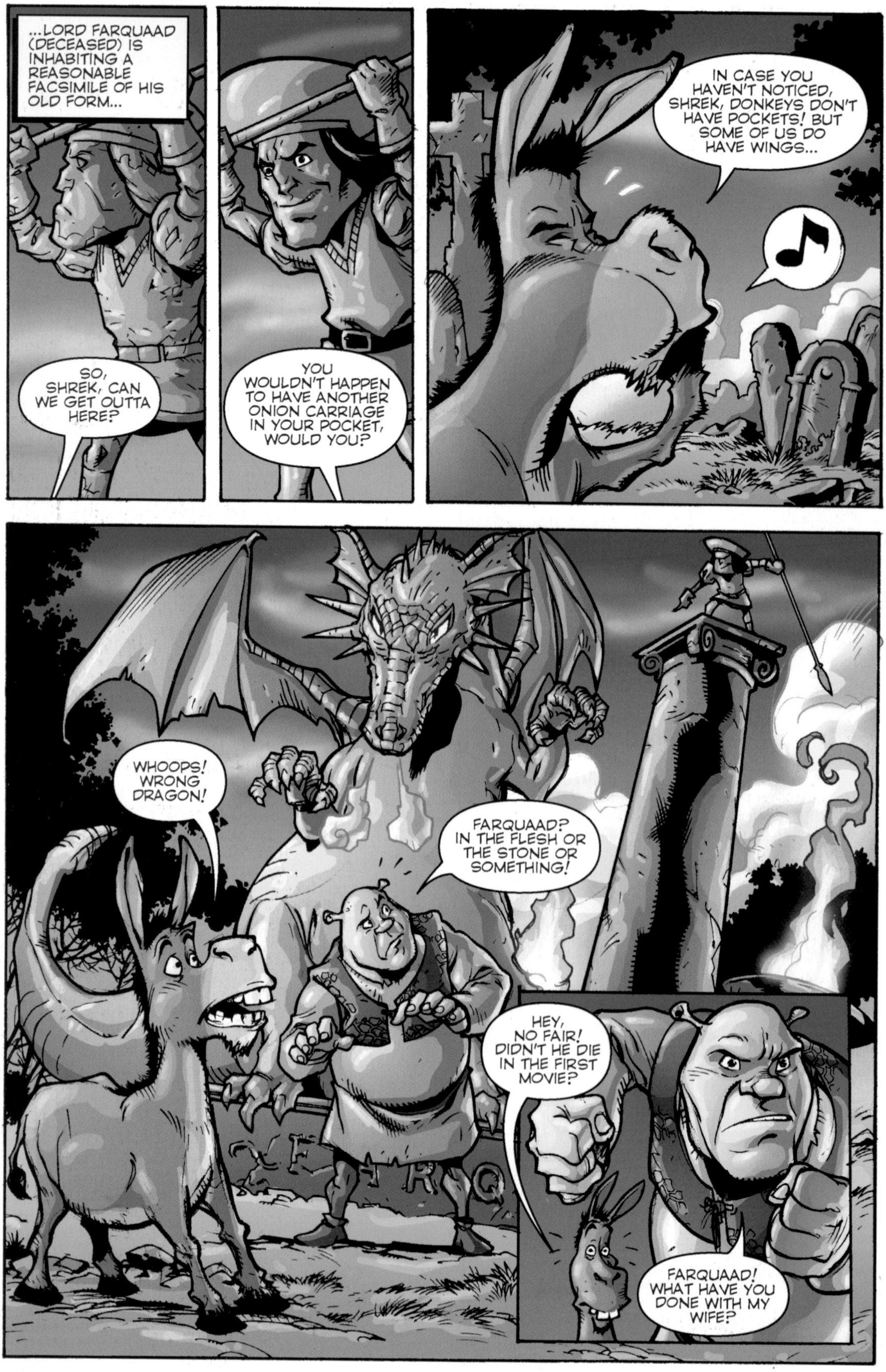
...LORD FARQUAAD (DECEASED) IS INHABITING A REASONABLE FACSIMILE OF HIS OLD FORM...
SO, SHREK, CAN WE GET OUTTA HERE?
YOU WOULDN'T HAPPEN TO HAVE ANOTHER ONION CARRIAGE IN YOUR POCKET, WOULD YOU?
IN CASE YOU HAVEN'T NOTICED, SHREK, DONKEYS DON'T HAVE POCKETS! BUT SOME OF US DO HAVE WINGS...
♪
WHOOPS! WRONG DRAGON!
FARQUAAD? IN THE FLESH OR THE STONE OR SOMETHING!
HEY, NO FAIR! DIDN'T HE DIE IN THE FIRST MOVIE?
FARQUAAD! WHAT HAVE YOU DONE WITH MY WIFE?

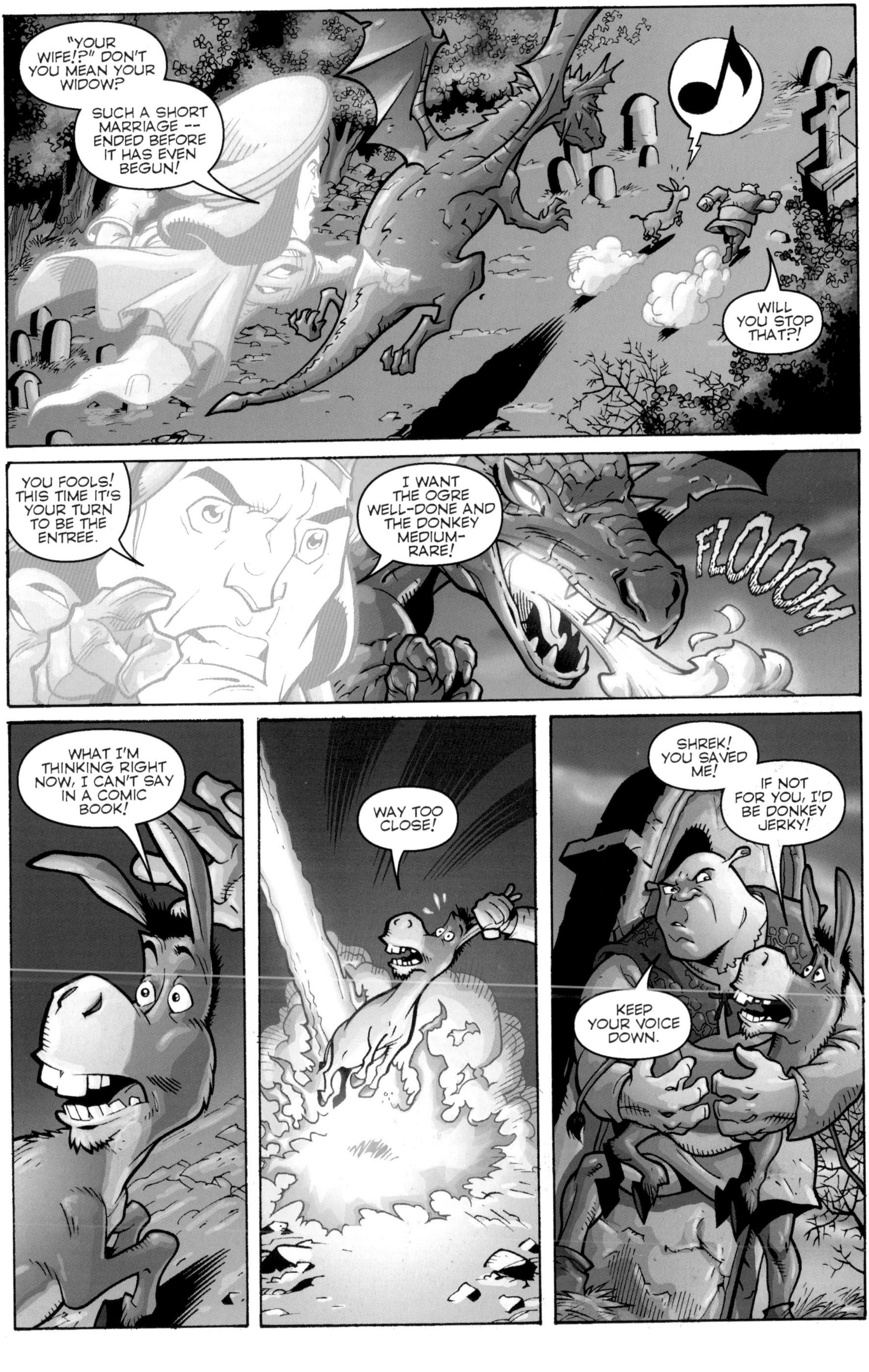
"YOUR WIFE!?" DON'T YOU MEAN YOUR WIDOW?
SUCH A SHORT MARRIAGE -- ENDED BEFORE IT HAS EVEN BEGUN!
WILL YOU STOP THAT?!
YOU FOOLS! THIS TIME IT'S YOUR TURN TO BE THE ENTREE.
I WANT THE OGRE WELL-DONE AND THE DONKEY MEDIUM-RARE!
FLOOOM
WHAT I'M THINKING RIGHT NOW, I CAN'T SAY IN A COMIC BOOK!
WAY TOO CLOSE!
SHREK! YOU SAVED ME!
IF NOT FOR YOU, I'D BE DONKEY JERKY!
KEEP YOUR VOICE DOWN.

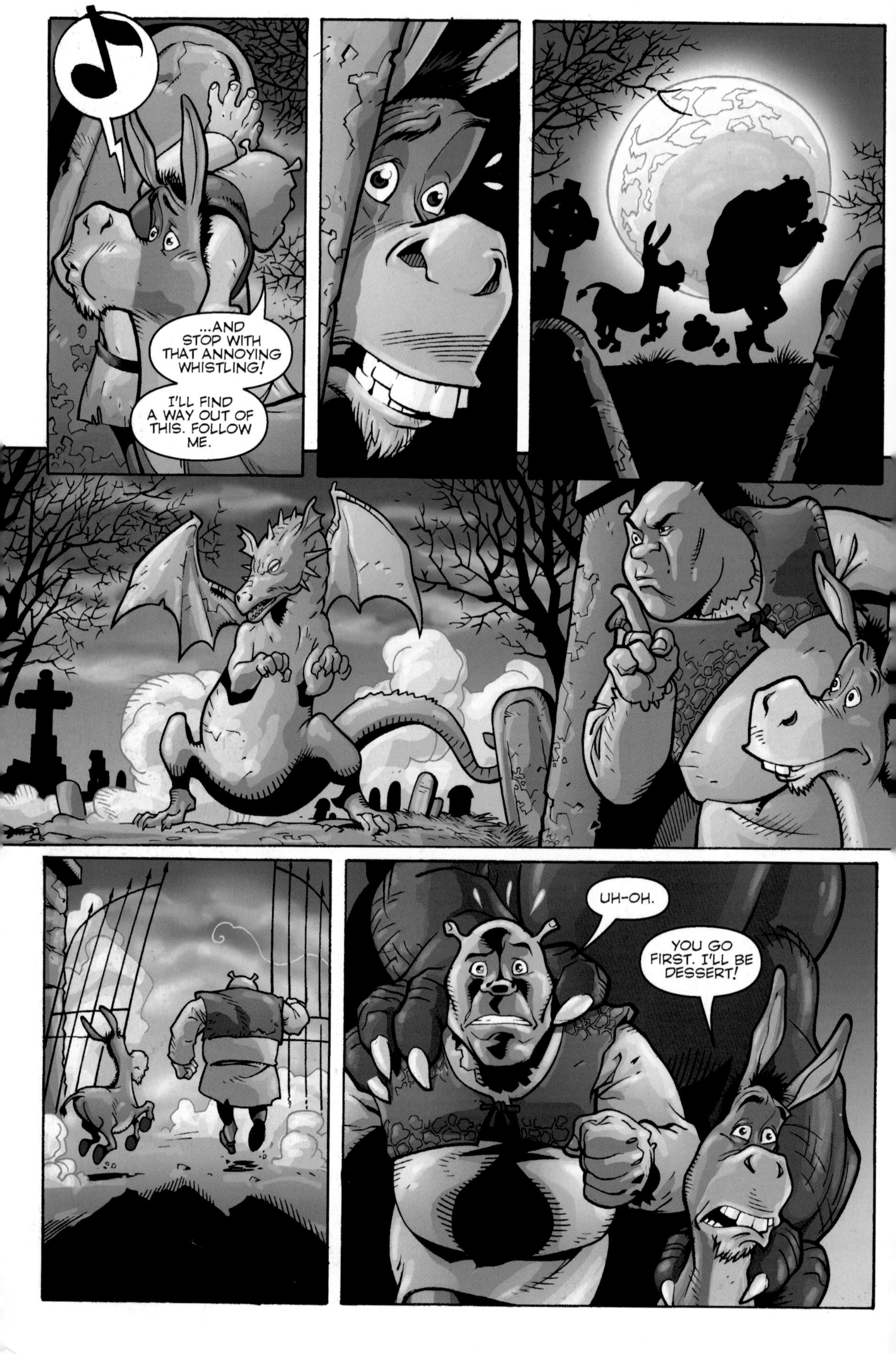
...AND STOP WITH THAT ANNOYING WHISTLING!
I'LL FIND A WAY OUT OF THIS. FOLLOW ME.
UH-OH.
YOU GO FIRST. I'LL BE DESSERT!

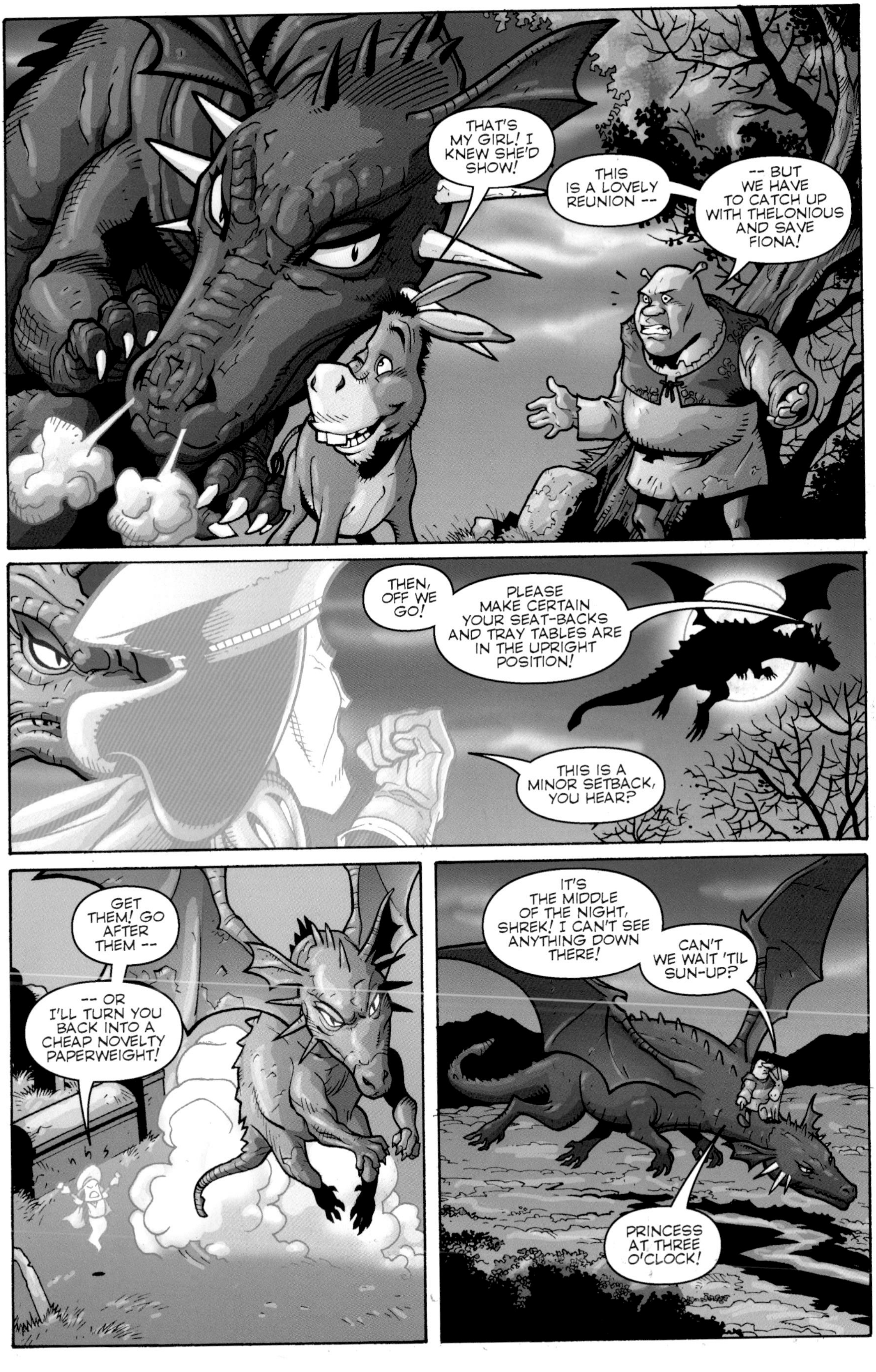
THAT'S MY GIRL! I KNEW SHE'D SHOW!
THIS IS A LOVELY REUNION --
-- BUT WE HAVE TO CATCH UP WITH THELONIOUS AND SAVE FIONA!
THEN, OFF WE GO!
PLEASE MAKE CERTAIN YOUR SEAT-BACKS AND TRAY TABLES ARE IN THE UPRIGHT POSITION!
THIS IS A MINOR SETBACK, YOU HEAR?
GET THEM! GO AFTER THEM --
-- OR I'LL TURN YOU BACK INTO A CHEAP NOVELTY PAPERWEIGHT!
IT'S THE MIDDLE OF THE NIGHT, SHREK! I CAN'T SEE ANYTHING DOWN THERE!
CAN'T WE WAIT 'TIL SUN-UP?
PRINCESS AT THREE O'CLOCK!

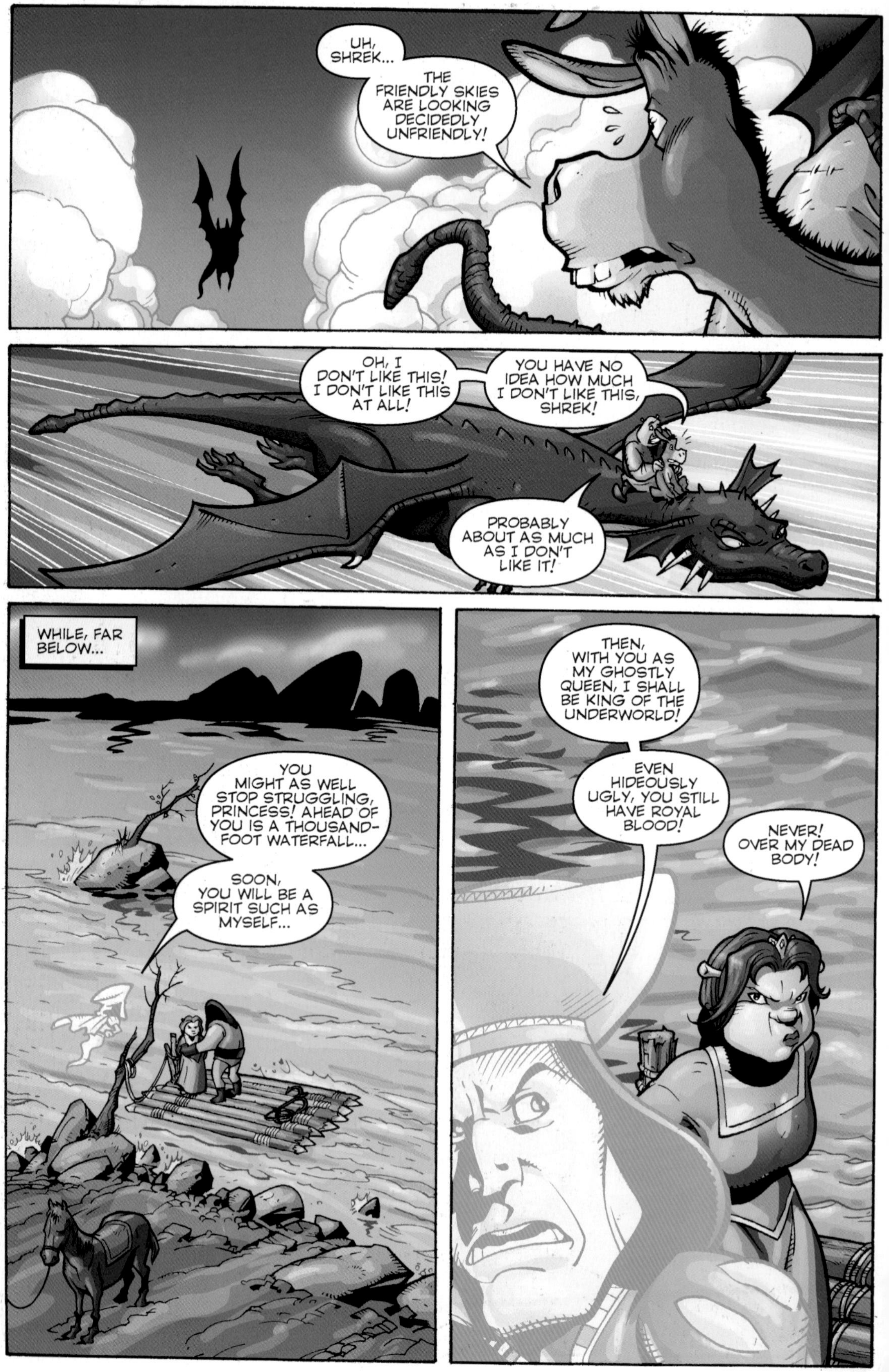
UH, SHREK...
THE FRIENDLY SKIES ARE LOOKING DECIDEDLY UNFRIENDLY!
OH, I DON'T LIKE THIS! I DON'T LIKE THIS AT ALL!
YOU HAVE NO IDEA HOW MUCH I DON'T LIKE THIS, SHREK!
PROBABLY ABOUT AS MUCH AS I DON'T LIKE IT!
WHILE, FAR BELOW...
YOU MIGHT AS WELL STOP STRUGGLING, PRINCESS! AHEAD OF YOU IS A THOUSAND-FOOT WATERFALL...
SOON, YOU WILL BE A SPIRIT SUCH AS MYSELF...
THEN, WITH YOU AS MY GHOSTLY QUEEN, I SHALL BE KING OF THE UNDERWORLD!
EVEN HIDEOUSLY UGLY, YOU STILL HAVE ROYAL BLOOD!
NEVER! OVER MY DEAD BODY!

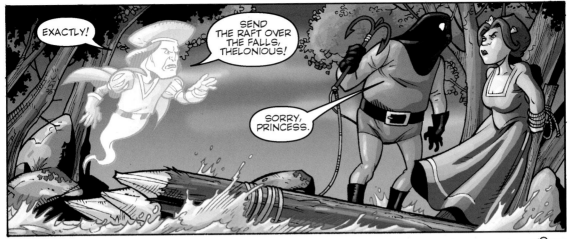

EXACTLY!

SEND THE RAFT OVER THE FALLS, THELONIOUS!

SORRY, PRINCESS.

YOU IMBECILE! NOT WITH YOU ON IT!

HUH?

IF YOU THINK I'M GOING TO WED THAT SAWED-OFF SPIRIT...

HEY, NO FAIR! YOU'RE SUPPOSED TO BE TIED-UP!

MAYBE I SHOULDN'T HAVE USED A SLIP-KNOT!

OOOF! SORRY. I DESERVED THAT.

WHUMP

KLUNK

AND THAT, TOO.

WHACK

AWWWW...

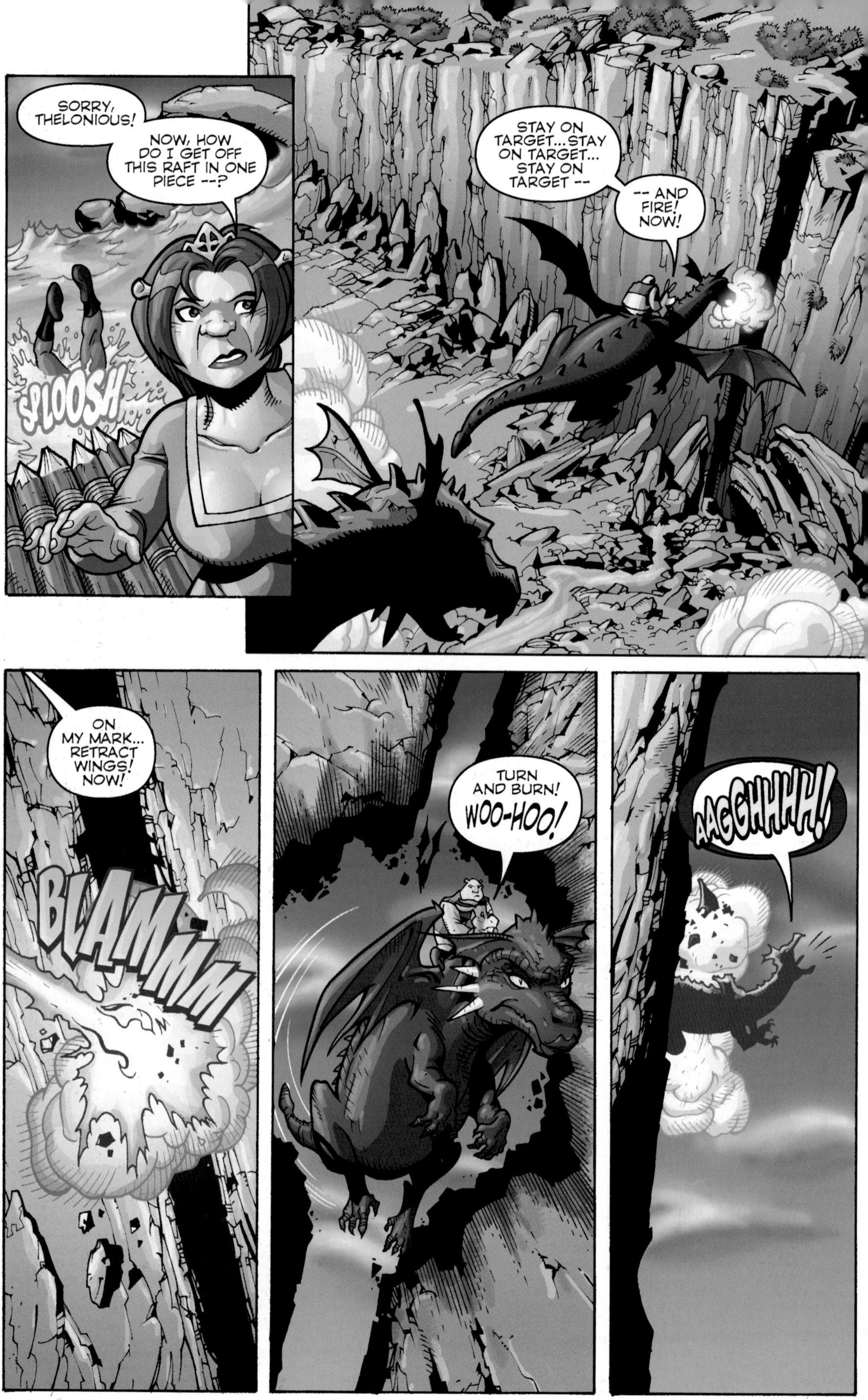
SORRY, THELONIOUS!
NOW, HOW DO I GET OFF THIS RAFT IN ONE PIECE --?
SPLOOSH
STAY ON TARGET...STAY ON TARGET... STAY ON TARGET --
-- AND FIRE! NOW!
ON MY MARK... RETRACT WINGS! NOW!
BLAMMM
TURN AND BURN! WOO-HOO!
AAGGHHHH!

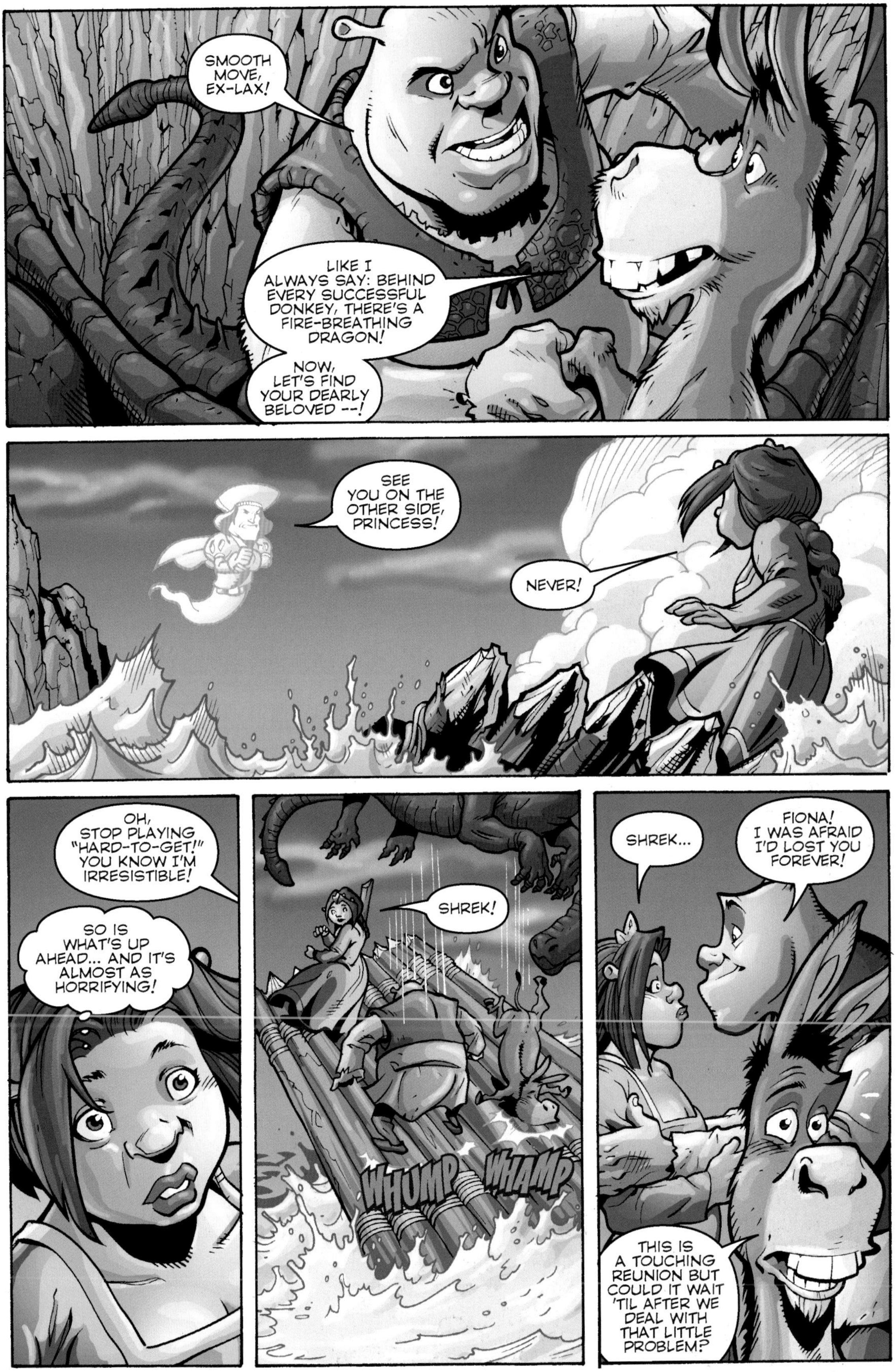
SMOOTH MOVE, EX-LAX!
LIKE I ALWAYS SAY: BEHIND EVERY SUCCESSFUL DONKEY, THERE'S A FIRE-BREATHING DRAGON!
NOW, LET'S FIND YOUR DEARLY BELOVED --!
SEE YOU ON THE OTHER SIDE, PRINCESS!
NEVER!
OH, STOP PLAYING "HARD-TO-GET!" YOU KNOW I'M IRRESISTIBLE!
SO IS WHAT'S UP AHEAD... AND IT'S ALMOST AS HORRIFYING!
SHREK!
WHUMP
WHAMP
SHREK...
FIONA! I WAS AFRAID I'D LOST YOU FOREVER!
THIS IS A TOUCHING REUNION BUT COULD IT WAIT 'TIL AFTER WE DEAL WITH THAT LITTLE PROBLEM?

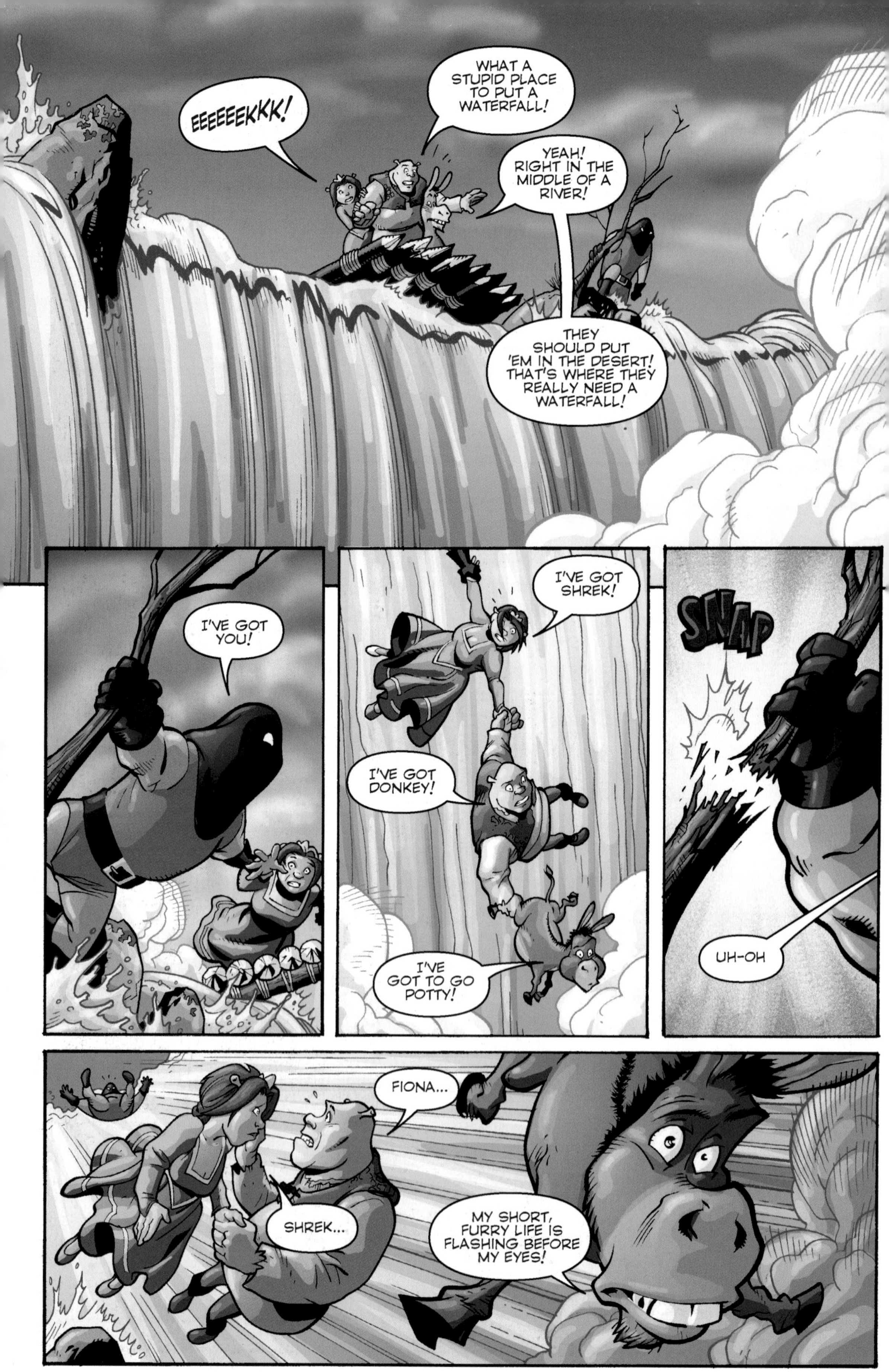
EEEEEEKKK!
WHAT A STUPID PLACE TO PUT A WATERFALL!
YEAH! RIGHT IN THE MIDDLE OF A RIVER!
THEY SHOULD PUT 'EM IN THE DESERT! THAT'S WHERE THEY REALLY NEED A WATERFALL!
I'VE GOT YOU!
I'VE GOT SHREK!
I'VE GOT DONKEY!
I'VE GOT TO GO POTTY!
SNAP
UH-OH
FIONA...
SHREK...
MY SHORT, FURRY LIFE IS FLASHING BEFORE MY EYES!

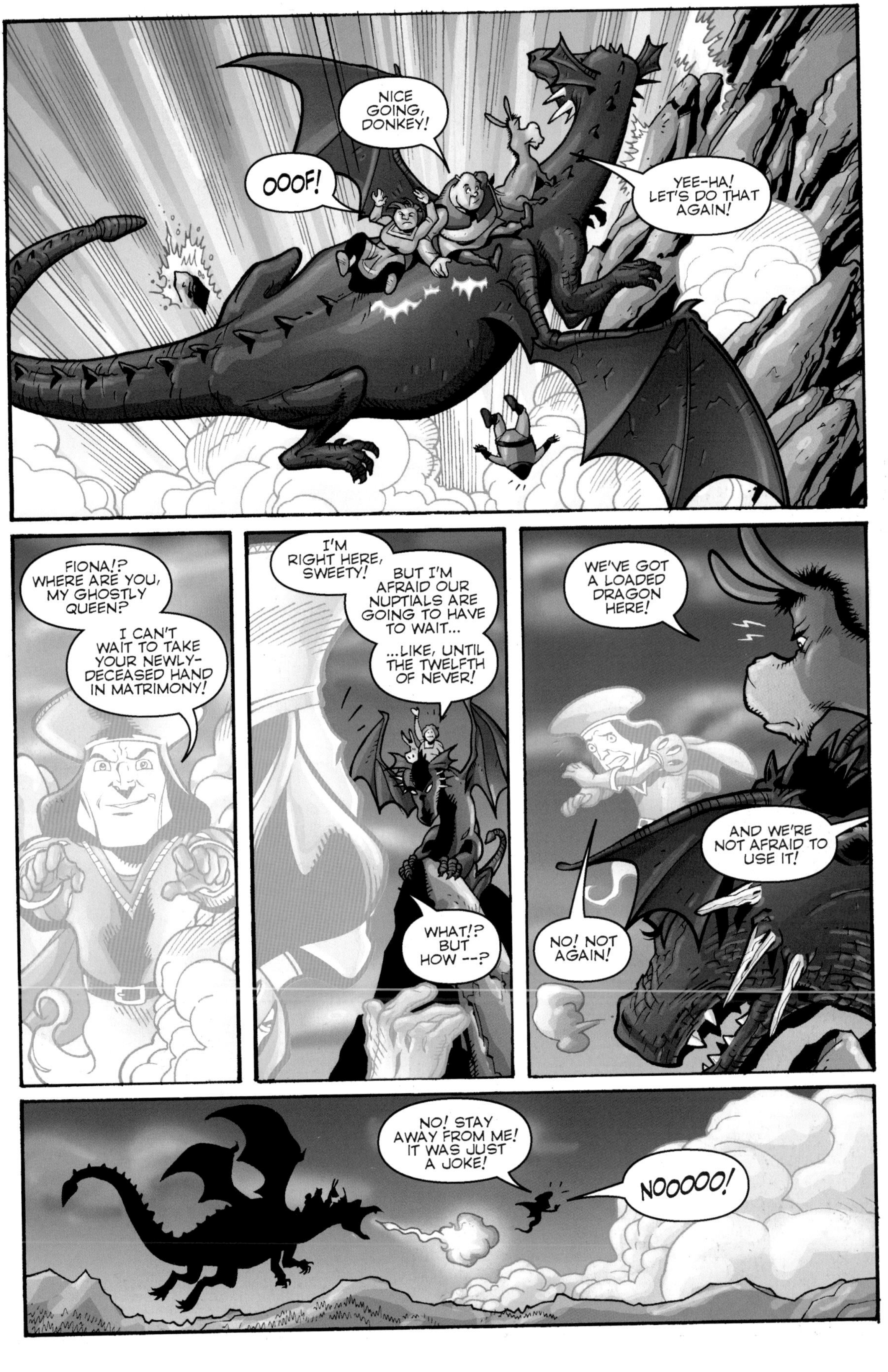
NICE GOING, DONKEY!
OOOF!
YEE-HA! LET'S DO THAT AGAIN!
FIONA!? WHERE ARE YOU, MY GHOSTLY QUEEN?
I CAN'T WAIT TO TAKE YOUR NEWLY-DECEASED HAND IN MATRIMONY!
I'M RIGHT HERE, SWEETY!
BUT I'M AFRAID OUR NUPTIALS ARE GOING TO HAVE TO WAIT...
...LIKE, UNTIL THE TWELFTH OF NEVER!
WHAT!? BUT HOW --?
WE'VE GOT A LOADED DRAGON HERE!
AND WE'RE NOT AFRAID TO USE IT!
NO! NOT AGAIN!
NO! STAY AWAY FROM ME! IT WAS JUST A JOKE!
NOOOOO!

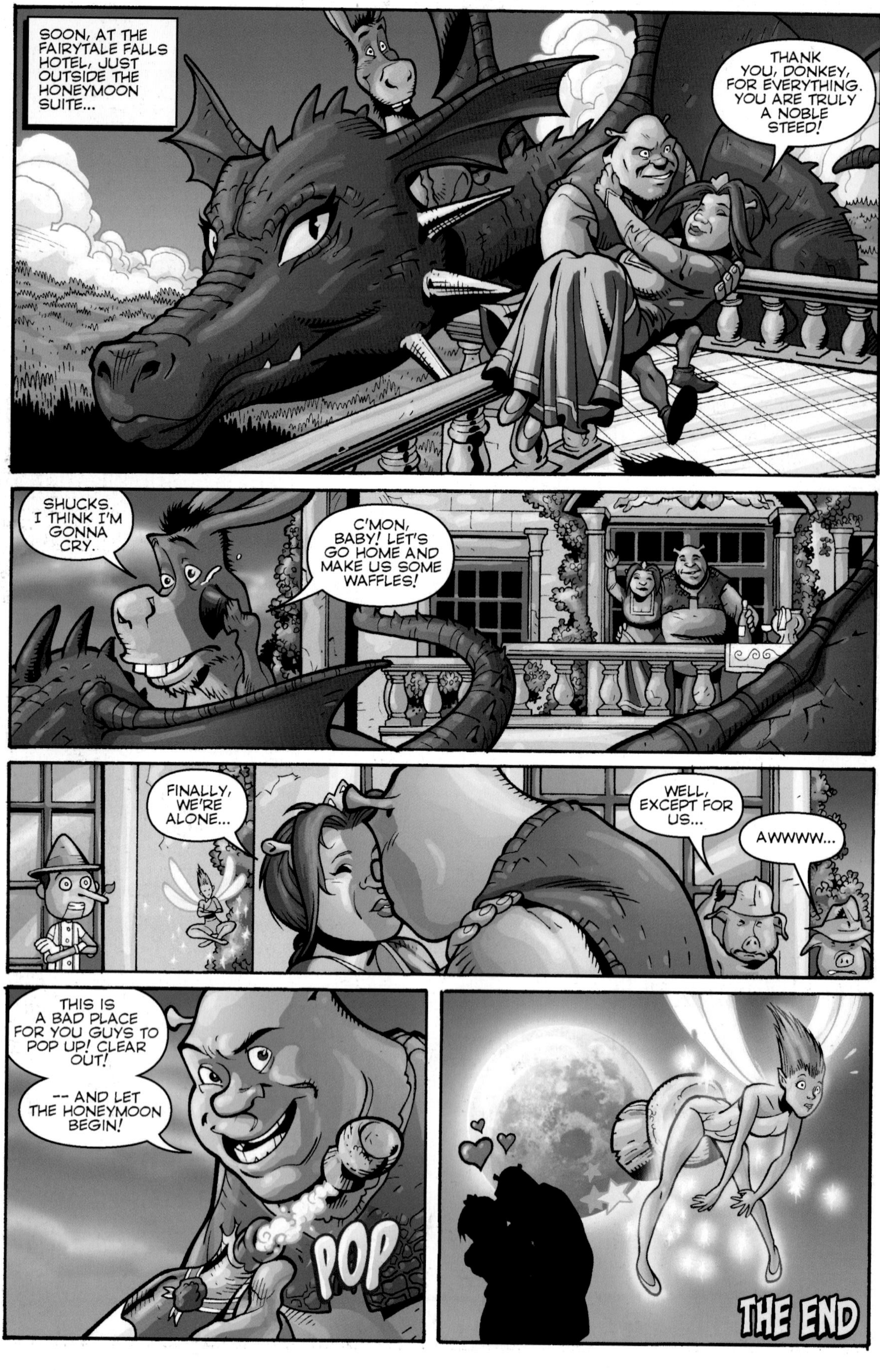
SOON, AT THE FAIRYTALE FALLS HOTEL, JUST OUTSIDE THE HONEYMOON SUITE...
THANK YOU, DONKEY, FOR EVERYTHING. YOU ARE TRULY A NOBLE STEED!
SHUCKS. I THINK I'M GONNA CRY.
C'MON, BABY! LET'S GO HOME AND MAKE US SOME WAFFLES!
FINALLY, WE'RE ALONE...
WELL, EXCEPT FOR US...
AWWWW...
THIS IS A BAD PLACE FOR YOU GUYS TO POP UP! CLEAR OUT!
-- AND LET THE HONEYMOON BEGIN!
POP
THE END

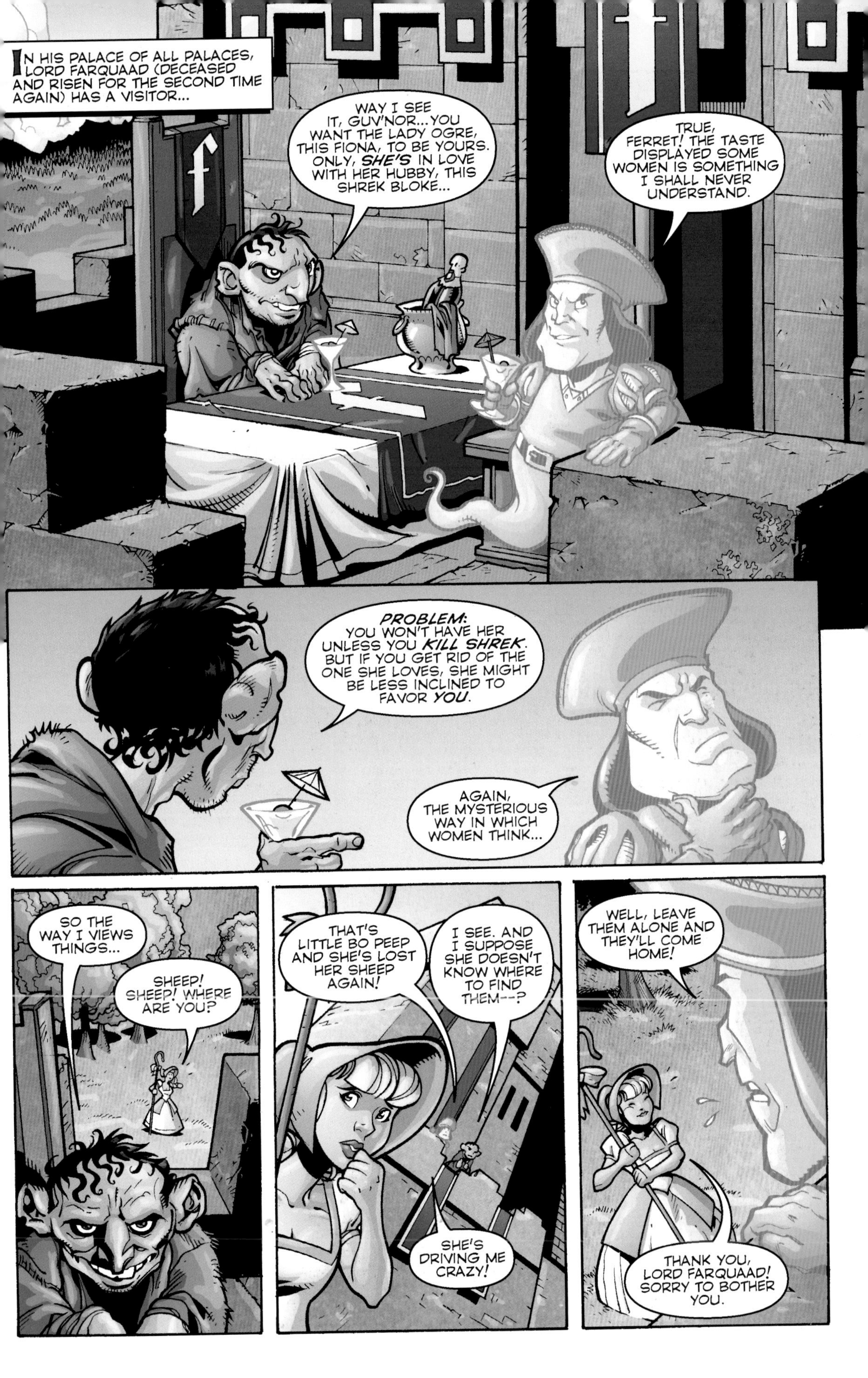
IN HIS PALACE OF ALL PALACES, LORD FARQUAAD (DECEASED AND RISEN FOR THE SECOND TIME AGAIN) HAS A VISITOR...
WAY I SEE IT, GUV'NOR... YOU WANT THE LADY OGRE, THIS FIONA, TO BE YOURS. ONLY, SHE'S IN LOVE WITH HER HUBBY, THIS SHREK BLOKE...
TRUE, FERRET! THE TASTE DISPLAYED SOME WOMEN IS SOMETHING I SHALL NEVER UNDERSTAND.
PROBLEM: YOU WON'T HAVE HER UNLESS YOU KILL SHREK. BUT IF YOU GET RID OF THE ONE SHE LOVES, SHE MIGHT BE LESS INCLINED TO FAVOR YOU.
AGAIN, THE MYSTERIOUS WAY IN WHICH WOMEN THINK...
SO THE WAY I VIEWS THINGS...
SHEEP! SHEEP! WHERE ARE YOU?
THAT'S LITTLE BO PEEP AND SHE'S LOST HER SHEEP AGAIN!
I SEE. AND I SUPPOSE SHE DOESN'T KNOW WHERE TO FIND THEM--?
SHE'S DRIVING ME CRAZY!
WELL, LEAVE THEM ALONE AND THEY'LL COME HOME!
THANK YOU, LORD FARQUAAD! SORRY TO BOTHER YOU.

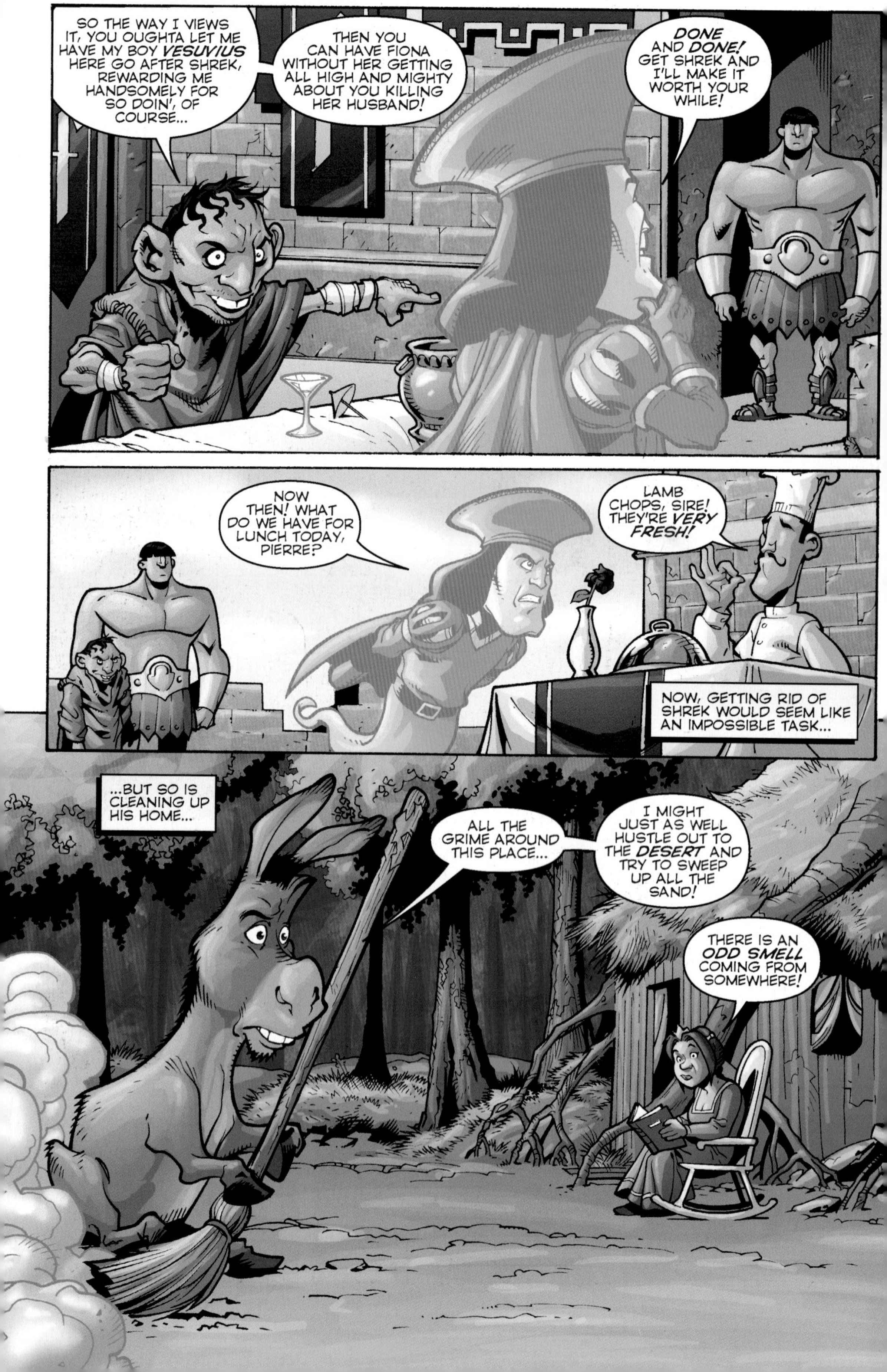
SO THE WAY I VIEWS IT, YOU OUGHTA LET ME HAVE MY BOY VESUVIUS HERE GO AFTER SHREK, REWARDING ME HANDSOMELY FOR SO DOIN', OF COURSE...
THEN YOU CAN HAVE FIONA WITHOUT HER GETTING ALL HIGH AND MIGHTY ABOUT YOU KILLING HER HUSBAND!
DONE AND DONE! GET SHREK AND I'LL MAKE IT WORTH YOUR WHILE!
NOW THEN! WHAT DO WE HAVE FOR LUNCH TODAY, PIERRE?
LAMB CHOPS, SIRE! THEY'RE VERY FRESH!
NOW, GETTING RID OF SHREK WOULD SEEM LIKE AN IMPOSSIBLE TASK...
...BUT SO IS CLEANING UP HIS HOME...
ALL THE GRIME AROUND THIS PLACE...
I MIGHT JUST AS WELL HUSTLE OUT TO THE DESERT AND TRY TO SWEEP UP ALL THE SAND!
THERE IS AN ODD SMELL COMING FROM SOMEWHERE!

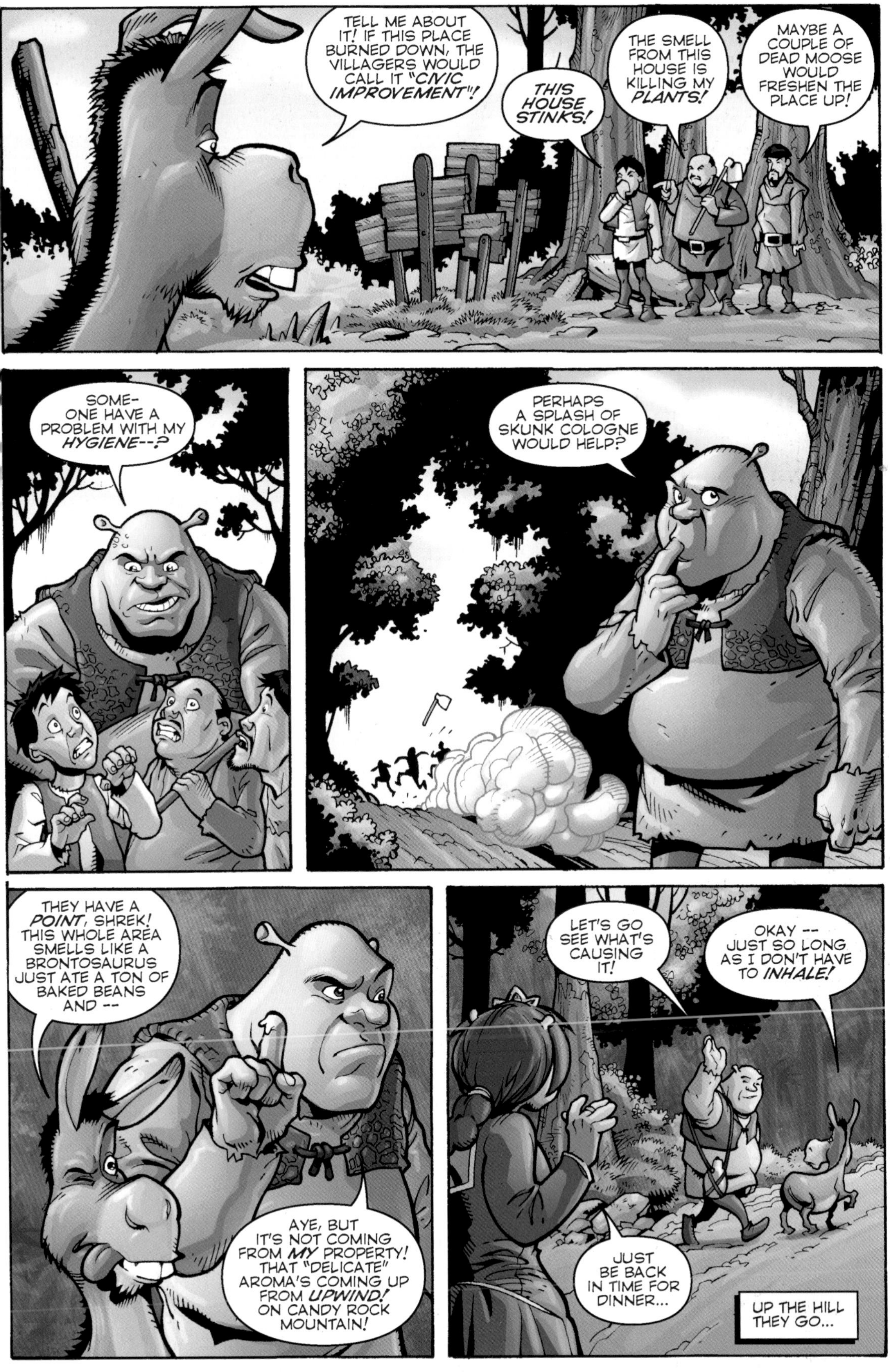
TELL ME ABOUT IT! IF THIS PLACE BURNED DOWN, THE VILLAGERS WOULD CALL IT "CIVIC IMPROVEMENT"!
THIS HOUSE STINKS!
THE SMELL FROM THIS HOUSE IS KILLING MY PLANTS!
MAYBE A COUPLE OF DEAD MOOSE WOULD FRESHEN THE PLACE UP!
SOME-ONE HAVE A PROBLEM WITH MY HYGIENE--?
PERHAPS A SPLASH OF SKUNK COLOGNE WOULD HELP?
THEY HAVE A POINT, SHREK! THIS WHOLE AREA SMELLS LIKE A BRONTOSAURUS JUST ATE A TON OF BAKED BEANS AND --
AYE, BUT IT'S NOT COMING FROM MY PROPERTY! THAT "DELICATE" AROMA'S COMING UP FROM UPWIND! ON CANDY ROCK MOUNTAIN!
LET'S GO SEE WHAT'S CAUSING IT!
OKAY -- JUST SO LONG AS I DON'T HAVE TO INHALE!
JUST BE BACK IN TIME FOR DINNER...
UP THE HILL THEY GO...

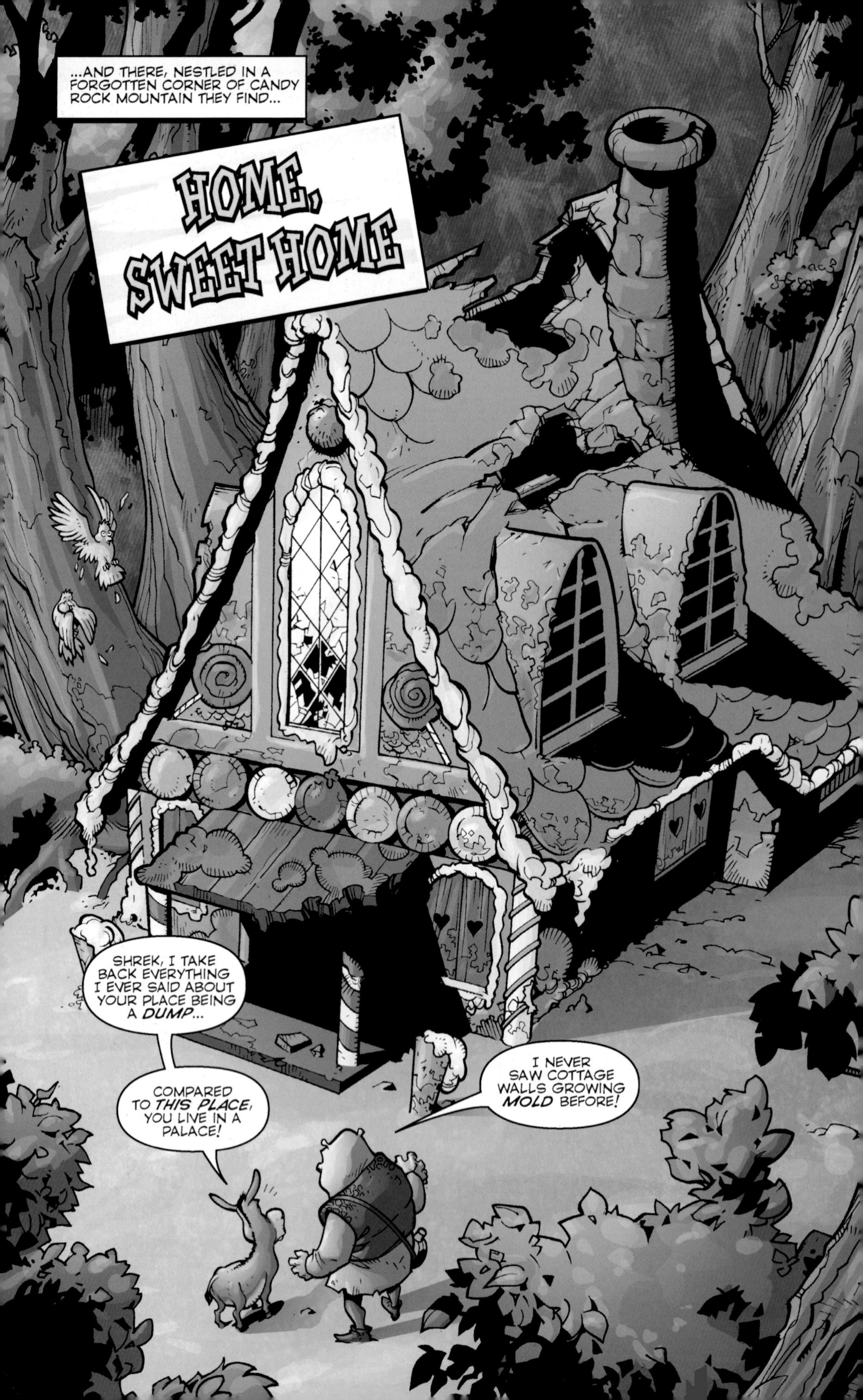
...AND THERE, NESTLED IN A FORGOTTEN CORNER OF CANDY ROCK MOUNTAIN THEY FIND...
HOME, SWEET HOME
SHREK, I TAKE BACK EVERYTHING I EVER SAID ABOUT YOUR PLACE BEING A DUMP...
COMPARED TO THIS PLACE, YOU LIVE IN A PALACE!
I NEVER SAW COTTAGE WALLS GROWING MOLD BEFORE!

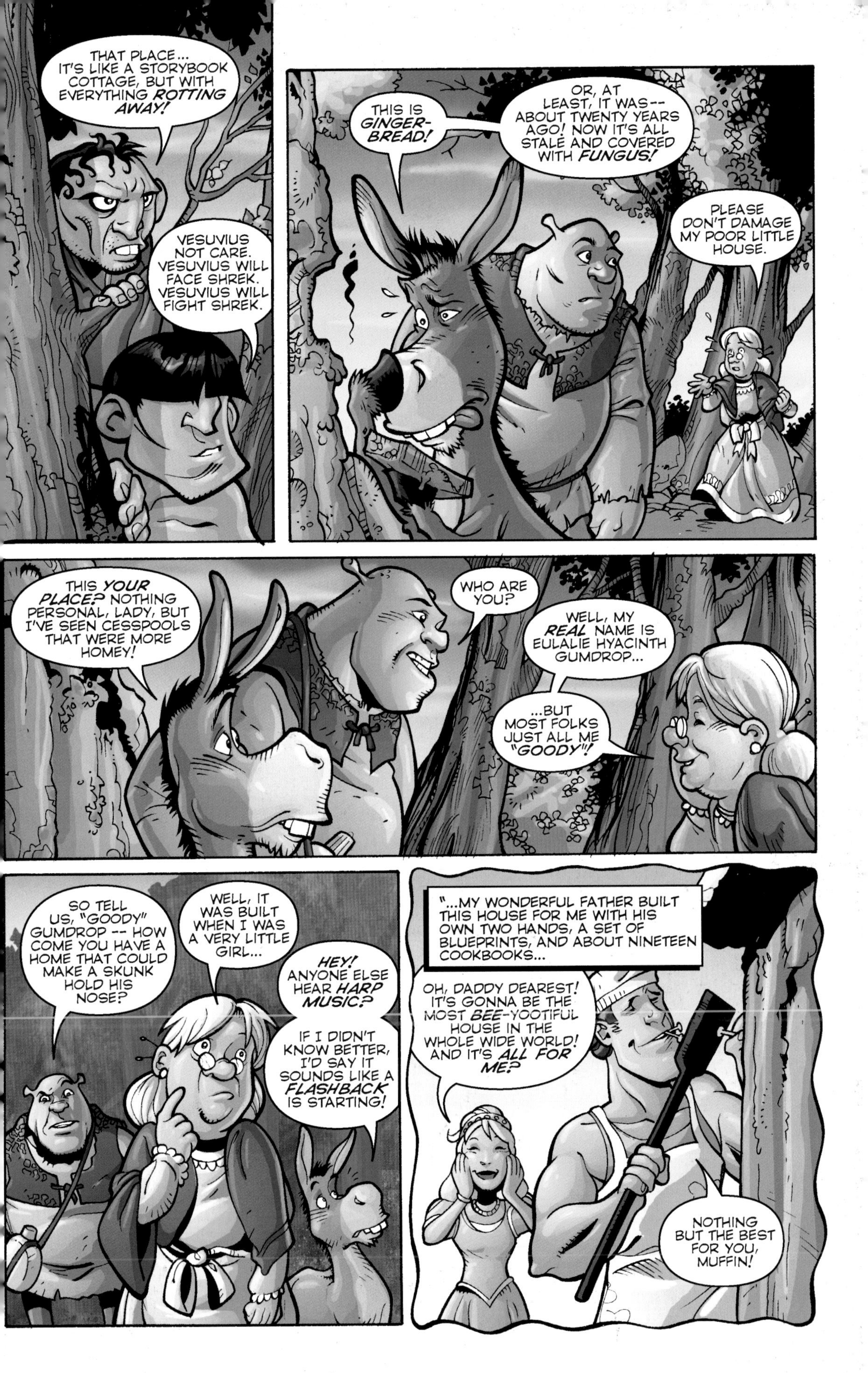
THAT PLACE... IT'S LIKE A STORYBOOK COTTAGE, BUT WITH EVERYTHING *ROTTING AWAY!*
VESUVIUS NOT CARE. VESUVIUS WILL FACE SHREK. VESUVIUS WILL FIGHT SHREK.
THIS IS *GINGER-BREAD!*
OR, AT LEAST, IT WAS-- ABOUT TWENTY YEARS AGO! NOW IT'S ALL STALE AND COVERED WITH *FUNGUS!*
PLEASE DON'T DAMAGE MY POOR LITTLE HOUSE.
THIS *YOUR PLACE?* NOTHING PERSONAL, LADY, BUT I'VE SEEN CESSPOOLS THAT WERE MORE HOMEY!
WHO ARE YOU?
WELL, MY *REAL* NAME IS EULALIE HYACINTH GUMDROP...
...BUT MOST FOLKS JUST ALL ME "*GOODY*"!
SO TELL US, "GOODY" GUMDROP -- HOW COME YOU HAVE A HOME THAT COULD MAKE A SKUNK HOLD HIS NOSE?
WELL, IT WAS BUILT WHEN I WAS A VERY LITTLE GIRL...
HEY! ANYONE ELSE HEAR *HARP MUSIC?*
IF I DIDN'T KNOW BETTER, I'D SAY IT SOUNDS LIKE A *FLASHBACK* IS STARTING!
"...MY WONDERFUL FATHER BUILT THIS HOUSE FOR ME WITH HIS OWN TWO HANDS, A SET OF BLUEPRINTS, AND ABOUT NINETEEN COOKBOOKS...
OH, DADDY DEAREST! IT'S GONNA BE THE MOST *BEE*-YOOTIFUL HOUSE IN THE WHOLE WIDE WORLD! AND IT'S *ALL FOR ME?*
NOTHING BUT THE BEST FOR YOU, MUFFIN!

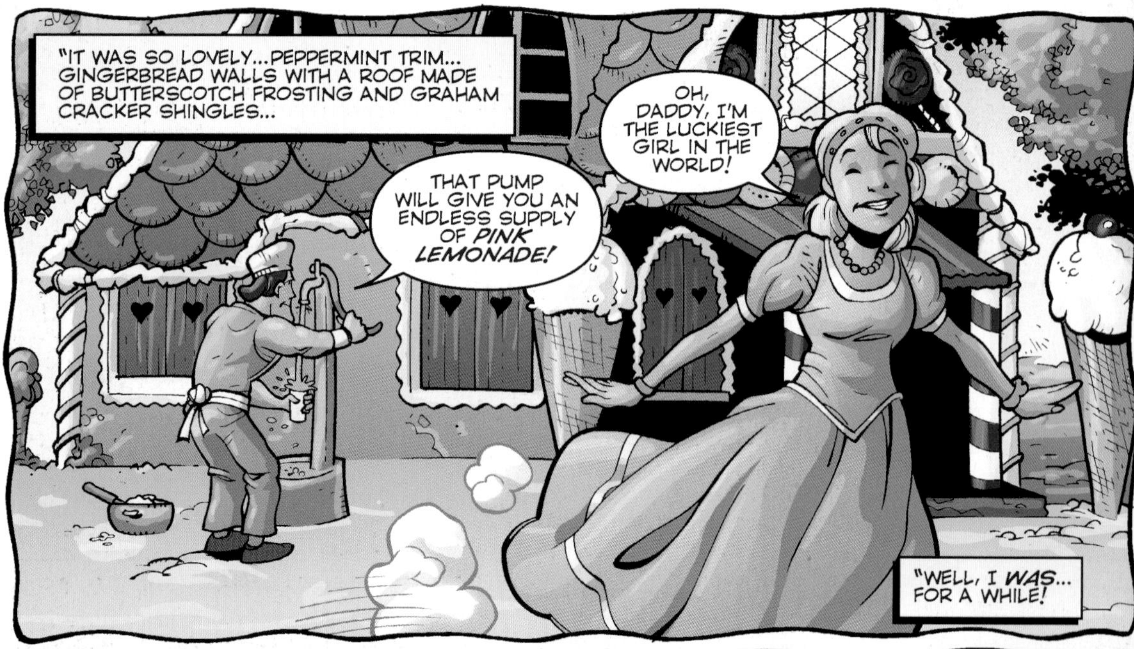
"IT WAS SO LOVELY...PEPPERMINT TRIM... GINGERBREAD WALLS WITH A ROOF MADE OF BUTTERSCOTCH FROSTING AND GRAHAM CRACKER SHINGLES...
THAT PUMP WILL GIVE YOU AN ENDLESS SUPPLY OF *PINK LEMONADE!*
OH, DADDY, I'M THE LUCKIEST GIRL IN THE WORLD!
"WELL, I *WAS*... FOR A WHILE!

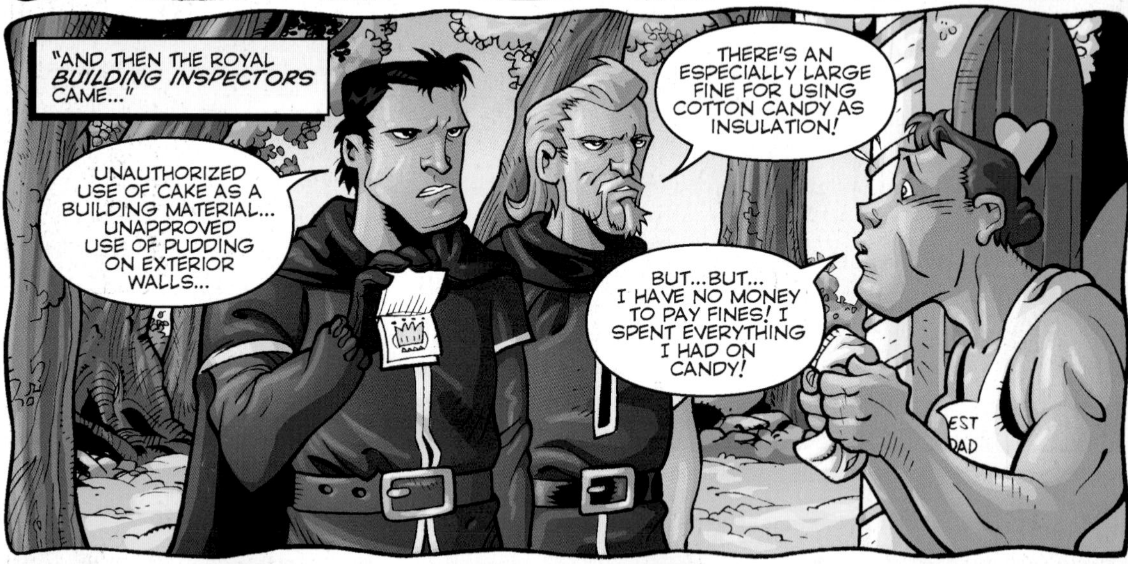
"AND THEN THE ROYAL *BUILDING INSPECTORS* CAME..."
UNAUTHORIZED USE OF CAKE AS A BUILDING MATERIAL... UNAPPROVED USE OF PUDDING ON EXTERIOR WALLS...
THERE'S AN ESPECIALLY LARGE FINE FOR USING COTTON CANDY AS INSULATION!
BUT...BUT... I HAVE NO MONEY TO PAY FINES! I SPENT EVERYTHING I HAD ON CANDY!

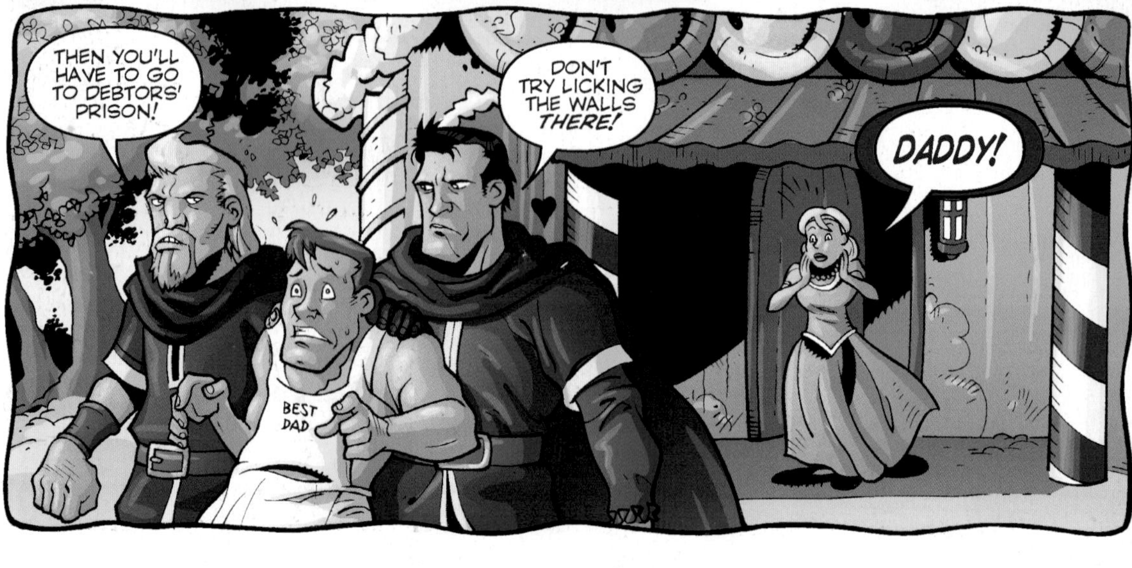
THEN YOU'LL HAVE TO GO TO DEBTORS' PRISON!
DON'T TRY LICKING THE WALLS *THERE!*
DADDY!
BEST DAD

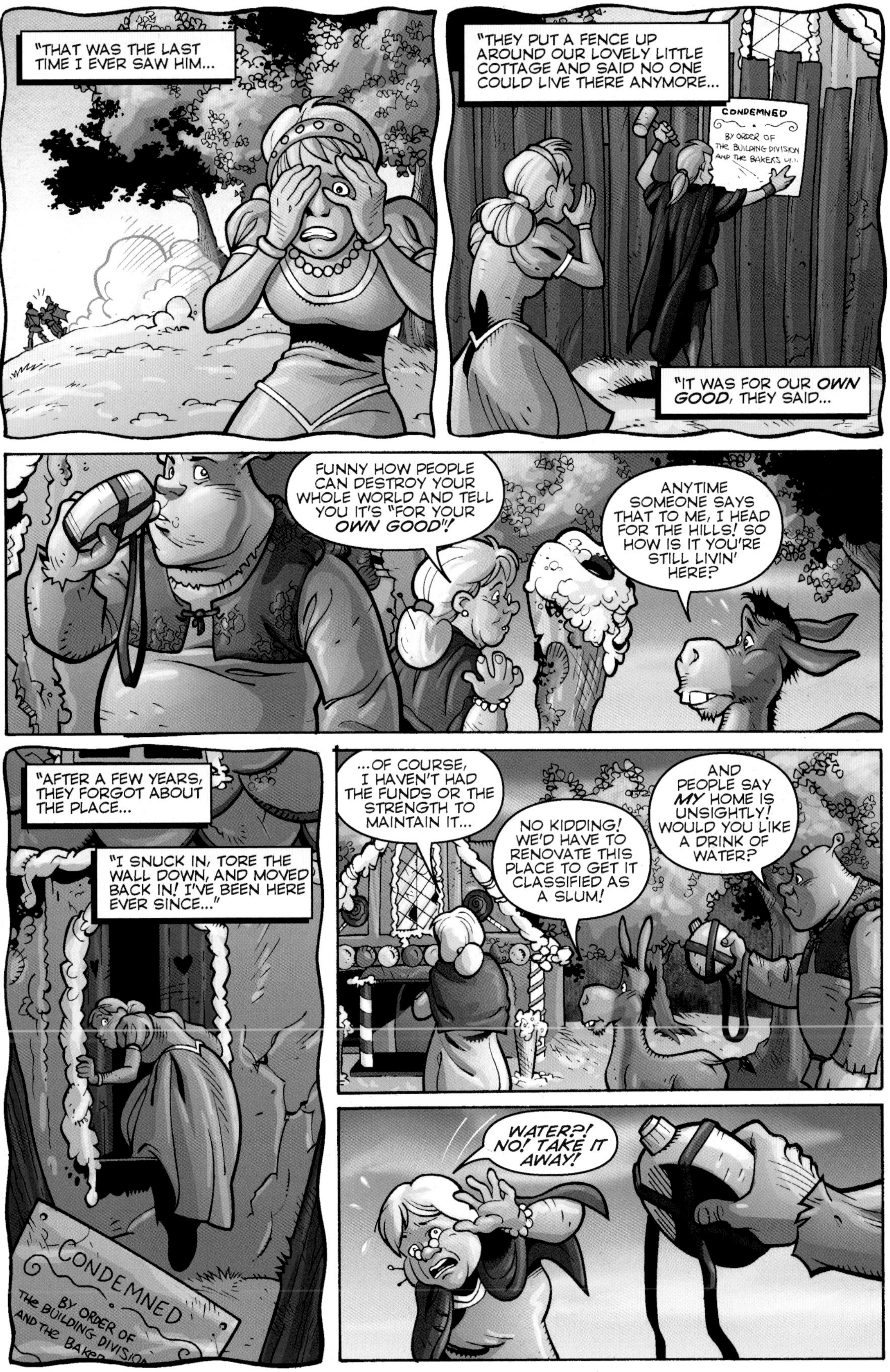
"THAT WAS THE LAST TIME I EVER SAW HIM...
"THEY PUT A FENCE UP AROUND OUR LOVELY LITTLE COTTAGE AND SAID NO ONE COULD LIVE THERE ANYMORE...
CONDEMNED
BY ORDER OF THE BUILDING DIVISION AND THE BAKER'S
"IT WAS FOR OUR *OWN GOOD*, THEY SAID...
FUNNY HOW PEOPLE CAN DESTROY YOUR WHOLE WORLD AND TELL YOU IT'S "FOR YOUR *OWN GOOD*"!
ANYTIME SOMEONE SAYS THAT TO ME, I HEAD FOR THE HILLS! SO HOW IS IT YOU'RE STILL LIVIN' HERE?
"AFTER A FEW YEARS, THEY FORGOT ABOUT THE PLACE...
"I SNUCK IN, TORE THE WALL DOWN, AND MOVED BACK IN! I'VE BEEN HERE EVER SINCE..."
CONDEMNED
BY ORDER OF THE BUILDING DIVISION AND THE
...OF COURSE, I HAVEN'T HAD THE FUNDS OR THE STRENGTH TO MAINTAIN IT...
NO KIDDING! WE'D HAVE TO RENOVATE THIS PLACE TO GET IT CLASSIFIED AS A SLUM!
AND PEOPLE SAY *MY* HOME IS UNSIGHTLY! WOULD YOU LIKE A DRINK OF WATER?
WATER?! NO! TAKE IT AWAY!

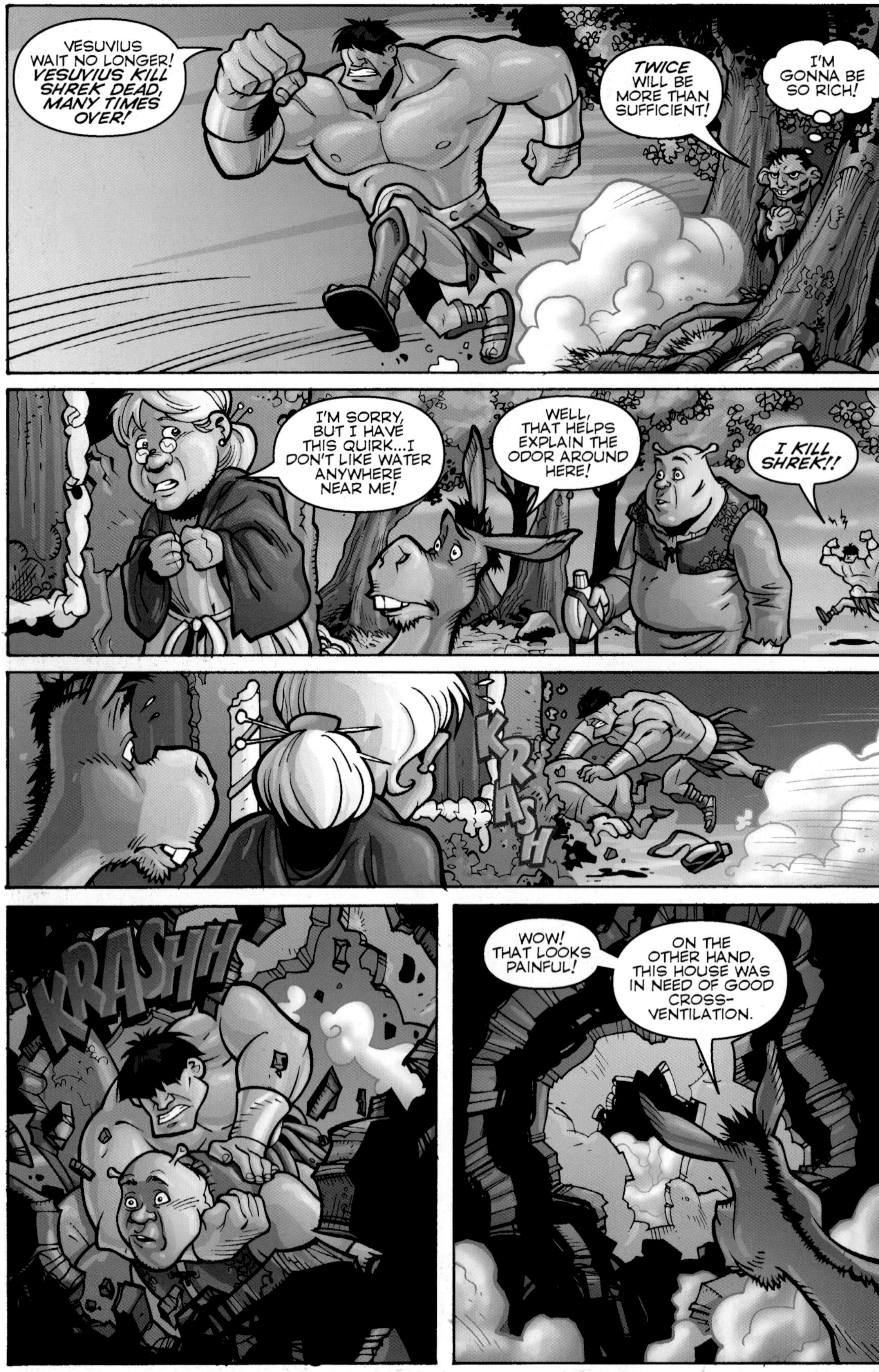
VESUVIUS WAIT NO LONGER! VESUVIUS KILL SHREK DEAD, MANY TIMES OVER!
TWICE WILL BE MORE THAN SUFFICIENT!
I'M GONNA BE SO RICH!
I'M SORRY, BUT I HAVE THIS QUIRK...I DON'T LIKE WATER ANYWHERE NEAR ME!
WELL, THAT HELPS EXPLAIN THE ODOR AROUND HERE!
I KILL SHREK!!
KRASH
KRASHH
WOW! THAT LOOKS PAINFUL!
ON THE OTHER HAND, THIS HOUSE WAS IN NEED OF GOOD CROSS-VENTILATION.

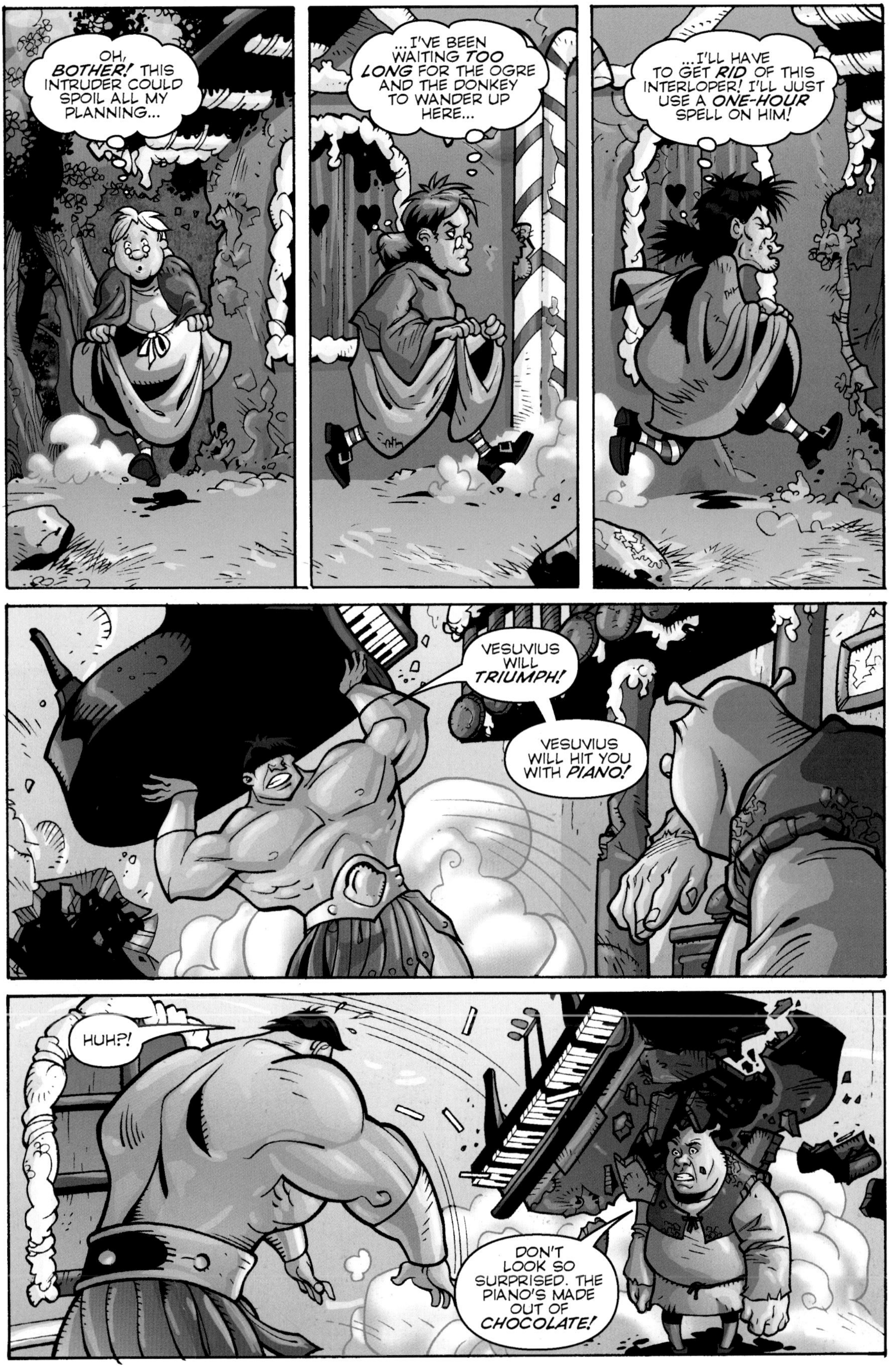
OH, BOTHER! THIS INTRUDER COULD SPOIL ALL MY PLANNING...
...I'VE BEEN WAITING TOO LONG FOR THE OGRE AND THE DONKEY TO WANDER UP HERE...
...I'LL HAVE TO GET RID OF THIS INTERLOPER! I'LL JUST USE A ONE-HOUR SPELL ON HIM!
VESUVIUS WILL TRIUMPH!
VESUVIUS WILL HIT YOU WITH PIANO!
HUH?!
DON'T LOOK SO SURPRISED. THE PIANO'S MADE OUT OF CHOCOLATE!

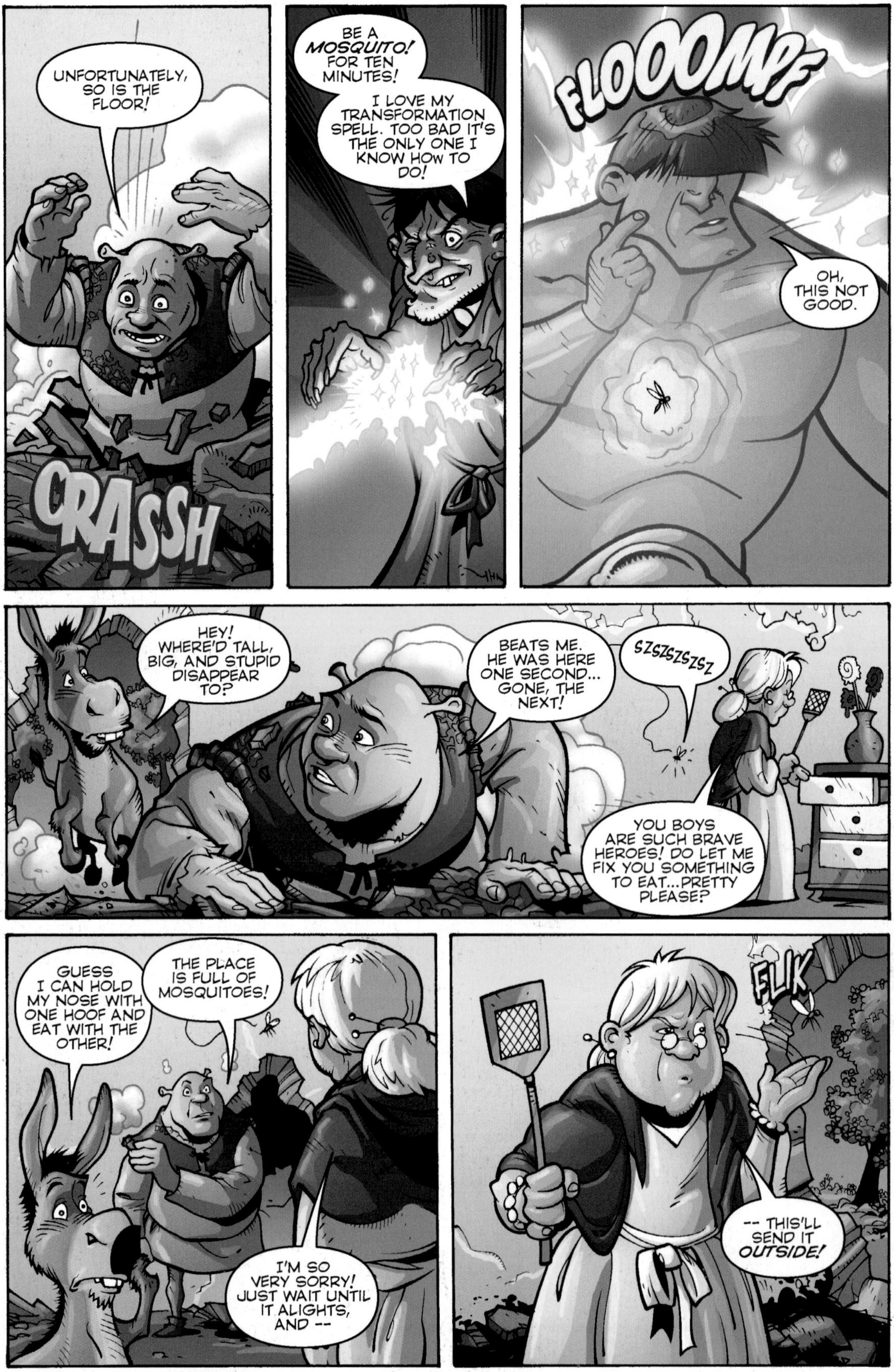
UNFORTUNATELY, SO IS THE FLOOR!
CRASSH
BE A MOSQUITO! FOR TEN MINUTES!
I LOVE MY TRANSFORMATION SPELL. TOO BAD IT'S THE ONLY ONE I KNOW HOW TO DO!
FLOOOMPF
OH, THIS NOT GOOD.
HEY! WHERE'D TALL, BIG, AND STUPID DISAPPEAR TO?
BEATS ME. HE WAS HERE ONE SECOND... GONE, THE NEXT!
SZSZSZSZSZ
YOU BOYS ARE SUCH BRAVE HEROES! DO LET ME FIX YOU SOMETHING TO EAT...PRETTY PLEASE?
GUESS I CAN HOLD MY NOSE WITH ONE HOOF AND EAT WITH THE OTHER!
THE PLACE IS FULL OF MOSQUITOES!
I'M SO VERY SORRY! JUST WAIT UNTIL IT ALIGHTS, AND --
FLIK
-- THIS'LL SEND IT OUTSIDE!

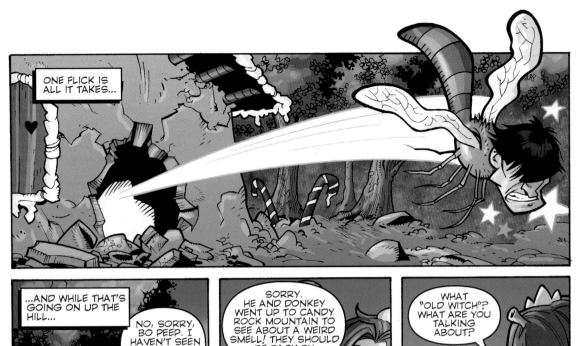

ONE FLICK IS ALL IT TAKES...

...AND WHILE THAT'S GOING ON UP THE HILL...

IS SHREK IN? COULD I ASK HIM?

NO, SORRY, BO PEEP. I HAVEN'T SEEN ANY SHEEP AROUND HERE!

SORRY. HE AND DONKEY WENT UP TO CANDY ROCK MOUNTAIN TO SEE ABOUT A WEIRD SMELL! THEY SHOULD BE BACK BY NOW.

NOT THE SMELL FROM THE OLD WITCH'S HOUSE?!

THEY DIDN'T GO UP THERE, DID THEY?

WHAT "OLD WITCH"? WHAT ARE YOU TALKING ABOUT?

DON'T YOU KNOW ABOUT HANSEL AND GRETEL AND THE OLD WITCH?

HANSEL AND GRETEL WERE THE TWO CHILDREN OF A LOCAL WOODCUTTER AND HIS WIFE...

"...THEY WERE OVERWEIGHT, SO THEIR MOTHER PUT THEM ON A STRICT DIET.

FROM NOW ON, NO SWEETS, NO STARCHES, NO FAT! YOU EAT ONLY TOFU!

"TOFU!?"

COULDN'T WE HAVE SOME FOOD INSTEAD?

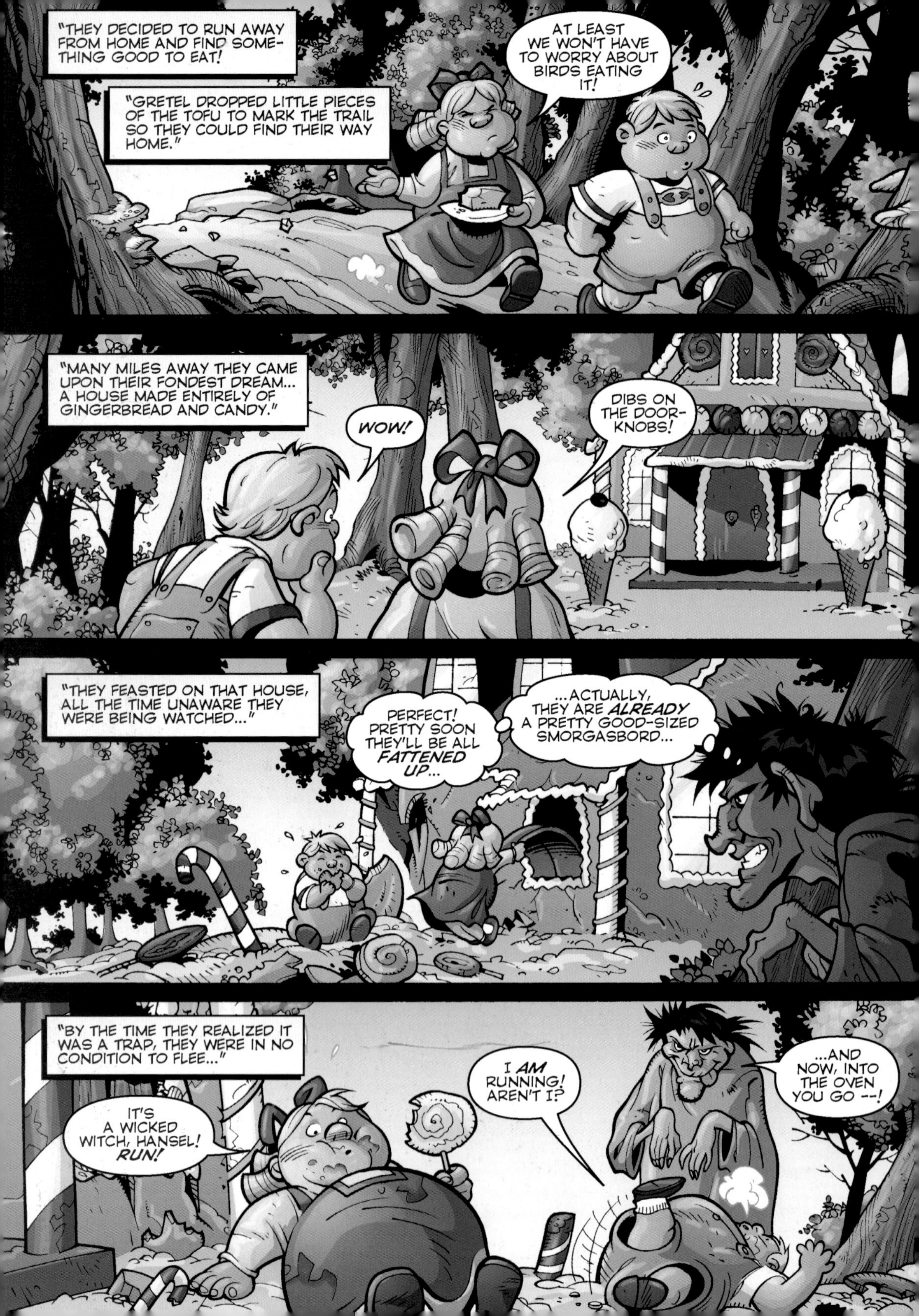
"THEY DECIDED TO RUN AWAY FROM HOME AND FIND SOMETHING GOOD TO EAT!
AT LEAST WE WON'T HAVE TO WORRY ABOUT BIRDS EATING IT!
"GRETEL DROPPED LITTLE PIECES OF THE TOFU TO MARK THE TRAIL SO THEY COULD FIND THEIR WAY HOME."
"MANY MILES AWAY THEY CAME UPON THEIR FONDEST DREAM... A HOUSE MADE ENTIRELY OF GINGERBREAD AND CANDY."
WOW!
DIBS ON THE DOOR-KNOBS!
"THEY FEASTED ON THAT HOUSE, ALL THE TIME UNAWARE THEY WERE BEING WATCHED..."
PERFECT! PRETTY SOON THEY'LL BE ALL FATTENED UP...
...ACTUALLY, THEY ARE ALREADY A PRETTY GOOD-SIZED SMORGASBORD...
"BY THE TIME THEY REALIZED IT WAS A TRAP, THEY WERE IN NO CONDITION TO FLEE..."
IT'S A WICKED WITCH, HANSEL! RUN!
I AM RUNNING! AREN'T I?
...AND NOW, INTO THE OVEN YOU GO --!

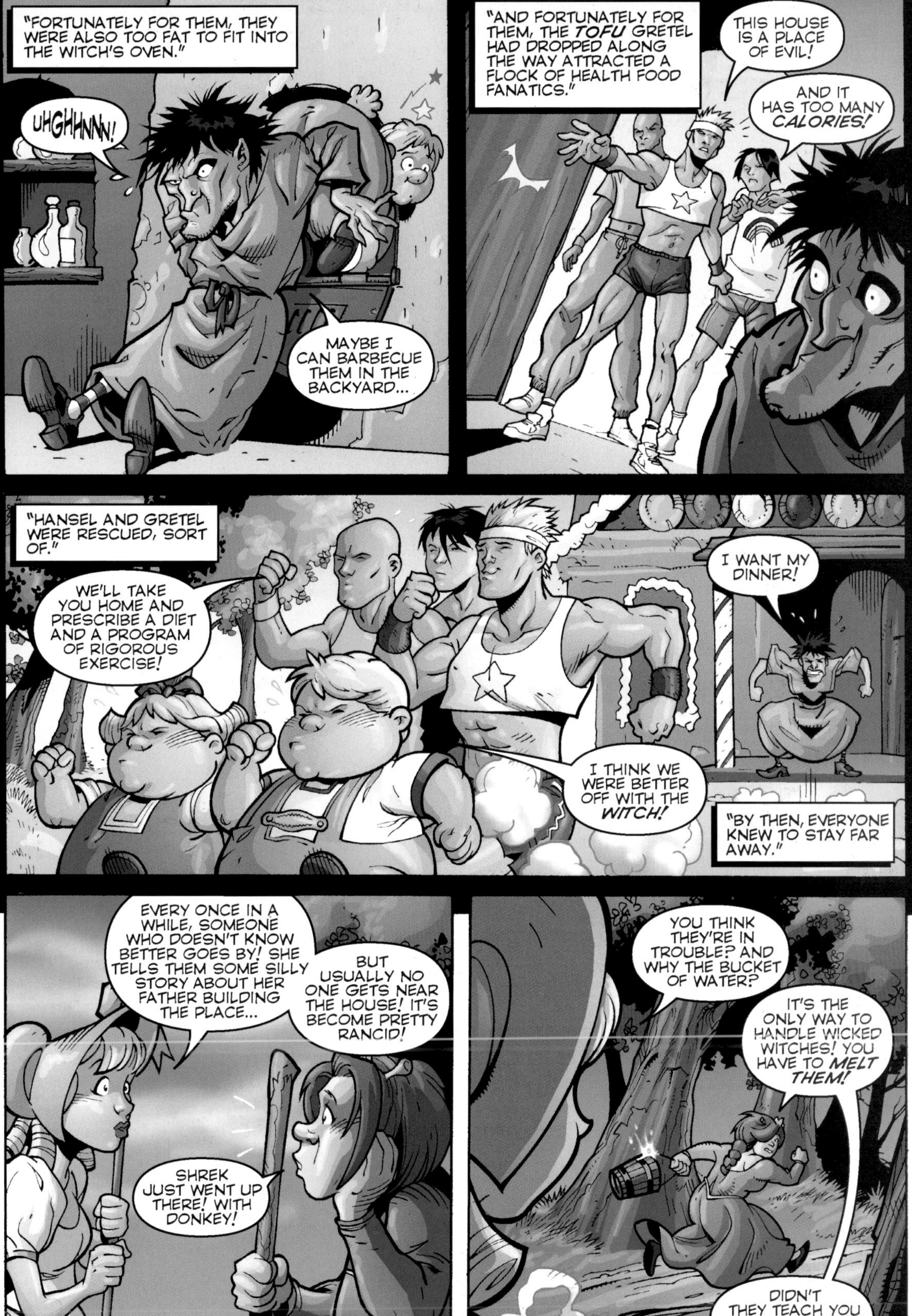
"FORTUNATELY FOR THEM, THEY WERE ALSO TOO FAT TO FIT INTO THE WITCH'S OVEN."
UHGHHNNN!
MAYBE I CAN BARBECUE THEM IN THE BACKYARD...
"AND FORTUNATELY FOR THEM, THE TOFU GRETEL HAD DROPPED ALONG THE WAY ATTRACTED A FLOCK OF HEALTH FOOD FANATICS."
THIS HOUSE IS A PLACE OF EVIL!
AND IT HAS TOO MANY CALORIES!
"HANSEL AND GRETEL WERE RESCUED, SORT OF."
WE'LL TAKE YOU HOME AND PRESCRIBE A DIET AND A PROGRAM OF RIGOROUS EXERCISE!
I WANT MY DINNER!
I THINK WE WERE BETTER OFF WITH THE WITCH!
"BY THEN, EVERYONE KNEW TO STAY FAR AWAY."
EVERY ONCE IN A WHILE, SOMEONE WHO DOESN'T KNOW BETTER GOES BY! SHE TELLS THEM SOME SILLY STORY ABOUT HER FATHER BUILDING THE PLACE...
BUT USUALLY NO ONE GETS NEAR THE HOUSE! IT'S BECOME PRETTY RANCID!
SHREK JUST WENT UP THERE! WITH DONKEY!
YOU THINK THEY'RE IN TROUBLE? AND WHY THE BUCKET OF WATER?
IT'S THE ONLY WAY TO HANDLE WICKED WITCHES! YOU HAVE TO MELT THEM!
DIDN'T THEY TEACH YOU ANYTHING IN SCHOOL?

OUTSIDE THE WITCH'S COTTAGE ARE TWO INSECTS -- FERRET AND A MOSQUITO...

SZSZSZSZSZ

I NEED VESUVIUS TO HELP ME GET RID OF SHREK! WHERE DID THAT IDIOT DISAPPEAR TO?

FLO OMP

SHE TURNED ME INTO A MOSQUITO, FERRET! SHE DID! SHE REALLY DID!

GET... OFF... ME.

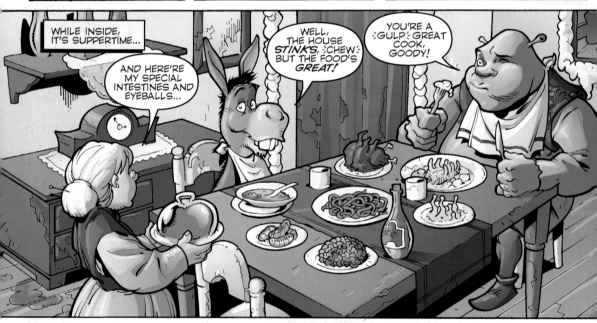

WHILE INSIDE, IT'S SUPPERTIME...

AND HERE'RE MY SPECIAL INTESTINES AND EYEBALLS...

WELL, THE HOUSE STINKS, ◦CHEW◦ BUT THE FOOD'S GREAT!

YOU'RE A ◦GULP◦ GREAT COOK, GOODY!

OH, THANK YOU. I DON'T GET MUCH COMPANY HERE.

CONSIDERING THE SMELL, THAT'S NOT ◦GULP◦ HARD TO EXPLAIN.

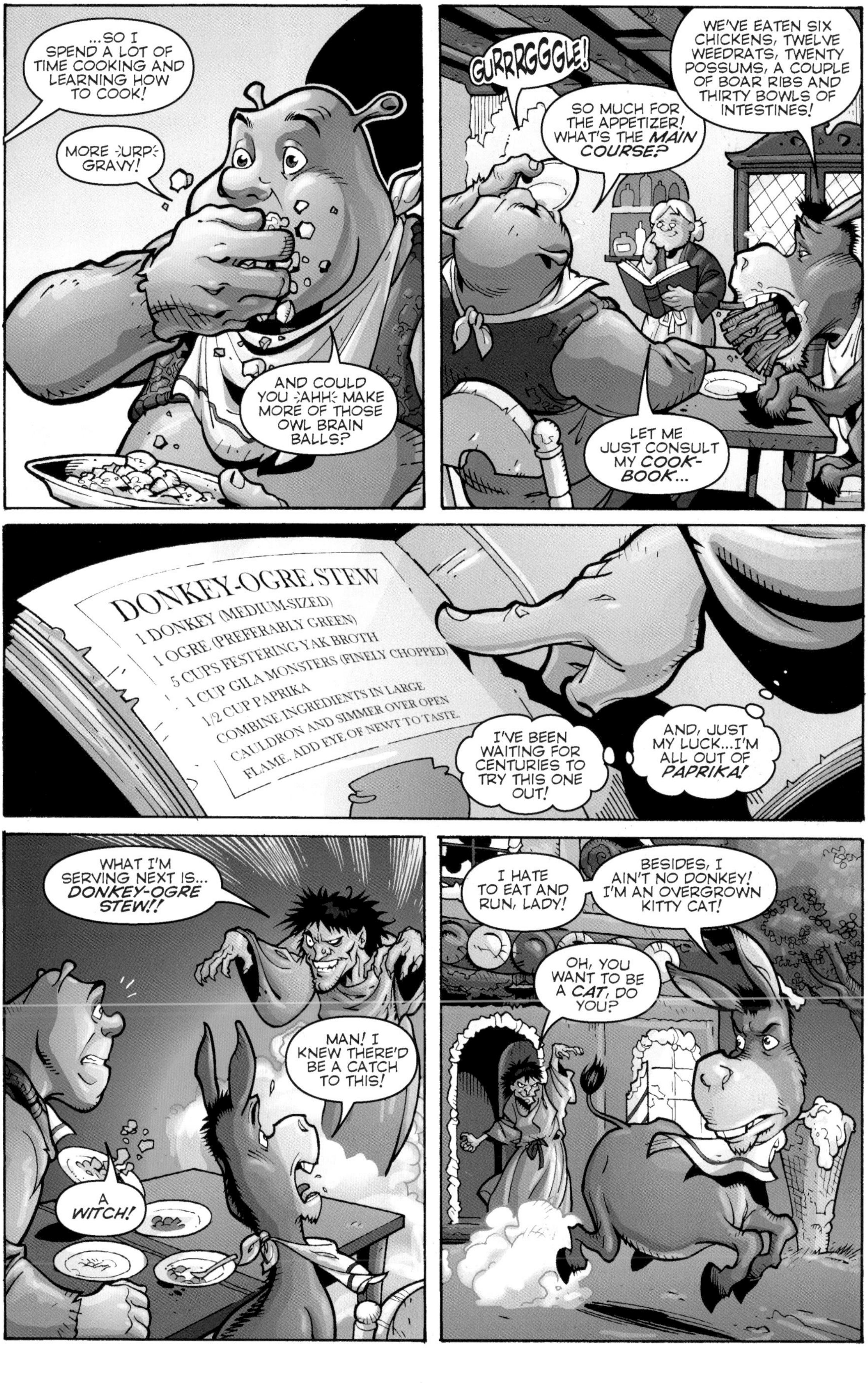
...SO I SPEND A LOT OF TIME COOKING AND LEARNING HOW TO COOK!
MORE -URP- GRAVY!
AND COULD YOU -AHH- MAKE MORE OF THOSE OWL BRAIN BALLS?
GURRRGGGLE!
WE'VE EATEN SIX CHICKENS, TWELVE WEEDRATS, TWENTY POSSUMS, A COUPLE OF BOAR RIBS AND THIRTY BOWLS OF INTESTINES!
SO MUCH FOR THE APPETIZER! WHAT'S THE MAIN COURSE?
LET ME JUST CONSULT MY COOK-BOOK...
DONKEY-OGRE STEW
1 DONKEY (MEDIUM-SIZED)
1 OGRE (PREFERABLY GREEN)
5 CUPS FESTERING YAK BROTH
1 CUP GILA MONSTERS (FINELY CHOPPED)
1/2 CUP PAPRIKA
COMBINE INGREDIENTS IN LARGE CAULDRON AND SIMMER OVER OPEN FLAME. ADD EYE OF NEWT TO TASTE.
I'VE BEEN WAITING FOR CENTURIES TO TRY THIS ONE OUT!
AND, JUST MY LUCK...I'M ALL OUT OF PAPRIKA!
WHAT I'M SERVING NEXT IS... DONKEY-OGRE STEW!!
MAN! I KNEW THERE'D BE A CATCH TO THIS!
A WITCH!
I HATE TO EAT AND RUN, LADY!
BESIDES, I AIN'T NO DONKEY! I'M AN OVERGROWN KITTY CAT!
OH, YOU WANT TO BE A CAT, DO YOU?

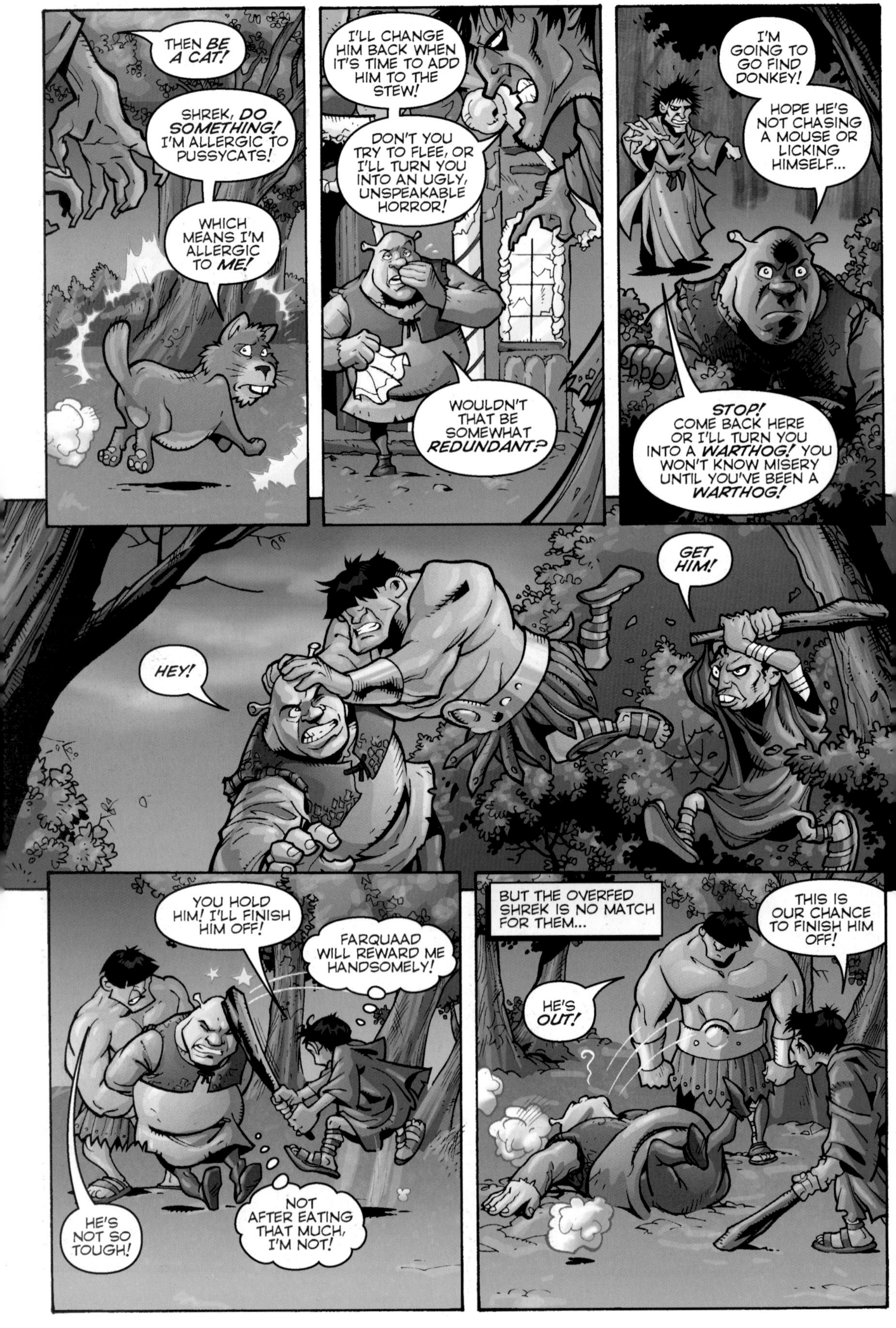
THEN BE A CAT!
SHREK, DO SOMETHING! I'M ALLERGIC TO PUSSYCATS!
WHICH MEANS I'M ALLERGIC TO ME!
I'LL CHANGE HIM BACK WHEN IT'S TIME TO ADD HIM TO THE STEW!
DON'T YOU TRY TO FLEE, OR I'LL TURN YOU INTO AN UGLY, UNSPEAKABLE HORROR!
WOULDN'T THAT BE SOMEWHAT REDUNDANT?
I'M GOING TO GO FIND DONKEY!
HOPE HE'S NOT CHASING A MOUSE OR LICKING HIMSELF...
STOP! COME BACK HERE OR I'LL TURN YOU INTO A WARTHOG! YOU WON'T KNOW MISERY UNTIL YOU'VE BEEN A WARTHOG!
GET HIM!
HEY!
YOU HOLD HIM! I'LL FINISH HIM OFF!
FARQUAAD WILL REWARD ME HANDSOMELY!
HE'S NOT SO TOUGH!
NOT AFTER EATING THAT MUCH, I'M NOT!
BUT THE OVERFED SHREK IS NO MATCH FOR THEM...
THIS IS OUR CHANCE TO FINISH HIM OFF!
HE'S OUT!

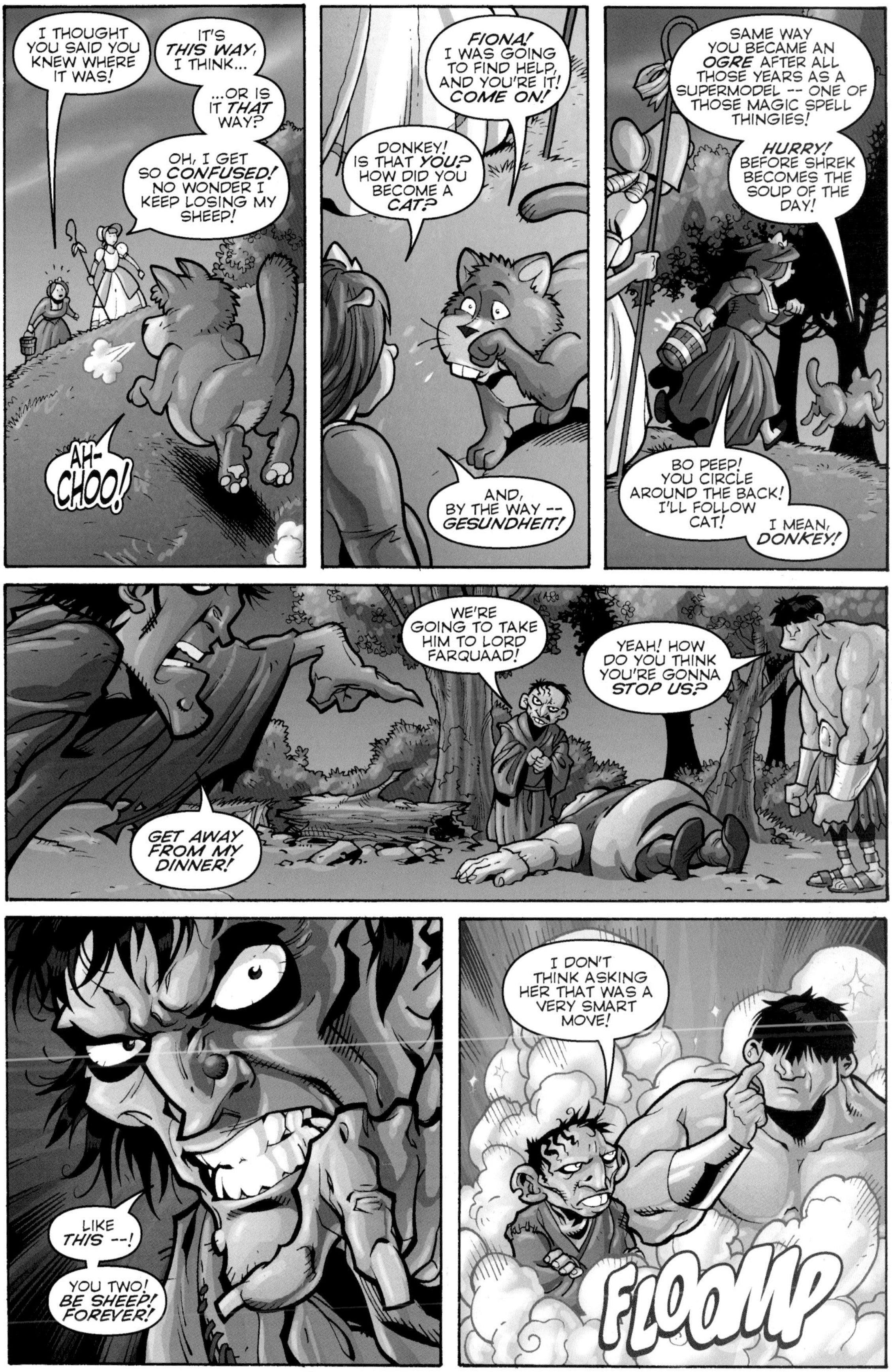
I THOUGHT YOU SAID YOU KNEW WHERE IT WAS!
IT'S THIS WAY, I THINK...
...OR IS IT THAT WAY?
OH, I GET SO CONFUSED! NO WONDER I KEEP LOSING MY SHEEP!
AH-CHOO!
FIONA! I WAS GOING TO FIND HELP, AND YOU'RE IT! COME ON!
DONKEY! IS THAT YOU? HOW DID YOU BECOME A CAT?
AND, BY THE WAY -- GESUNDHEIT!
SAME WAY YOU BECAME AN OGRE AFTER ALL THOSE YEARS AS A SUPERMODEL -- ONE OF THOSE MAGIC SPELL THINGIES!
HURRY! BEFORE SHREK BECOMES THE SOUP OF THE DAY!
BO PEEP! YOU CIRCLE AROUND THE BACK! I'LL FOLLOW CAT!
I MEAN, DONKEY!
GET AWAY FROM MY DINNER!
WE'RE GOING TO TAKE HIM TO LORD FARQUAAD!
YEAH! HOW DO YOU THINK YOU'RE GONNA STOP US?
LIKE THIS --!
YOU TWO! BE SHEEP! FOREVER!
I DON'T THINK ASKING HER THAT WAS A VERY SMART MOVE!
FLOOMP

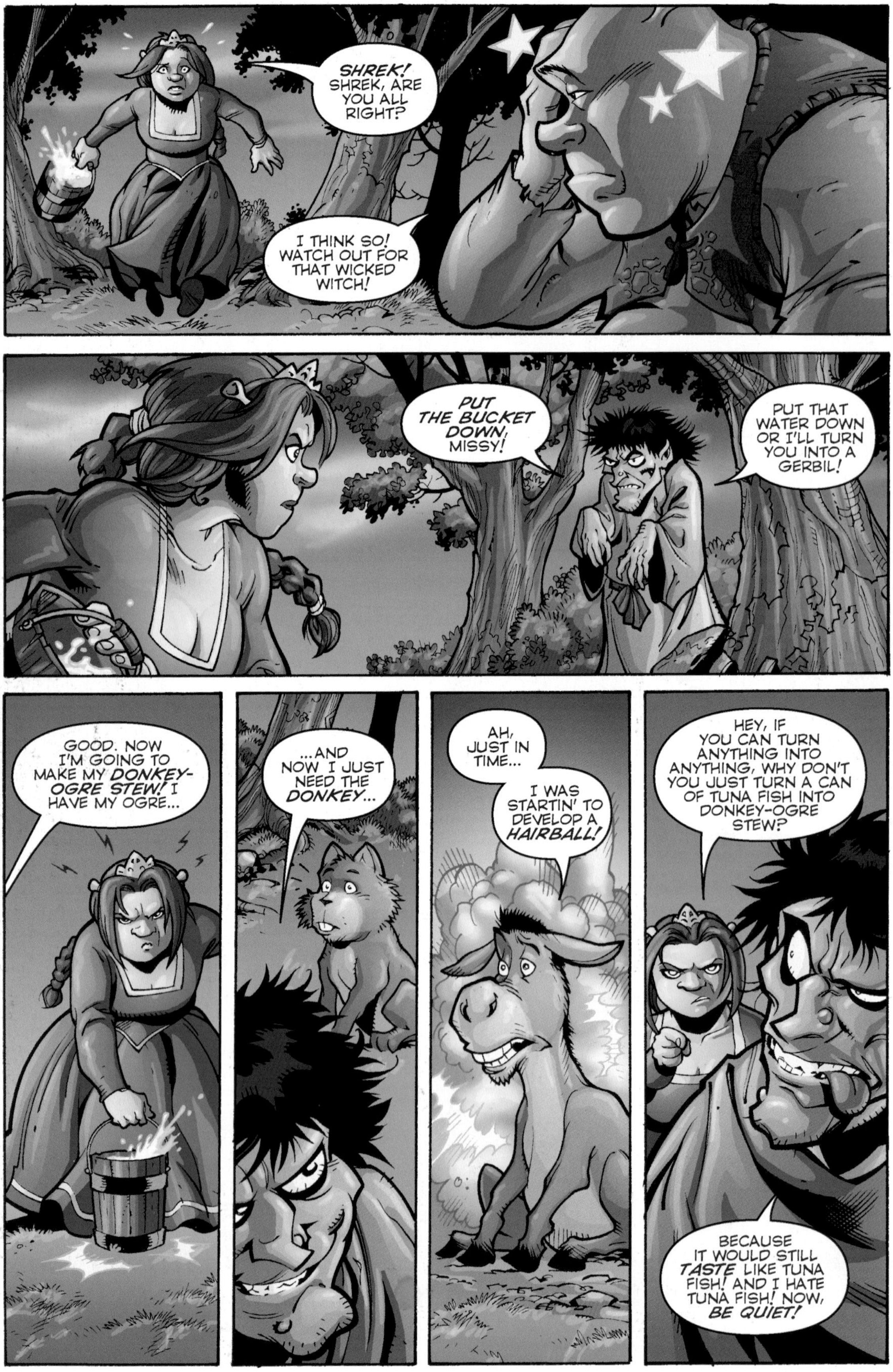
SHREK! SHREK, ARE YOU ALL RIGHT?
I THINK SO! WATCH OUT FOR THAT WICKED WITCH!
PUT THE BUCKET DOWN, MISSY!
PUT THAT WATER DOWN OR I'LL TURN YOU INTO A GERBIL!
GOOD. NOW I'M GOING TO MAKE MY DONKEY-OGRE STEW! I HAVE MY OGRE...
...AND NOW I JUST NEED THE DONKEY...
AH, JUST IN TIME...
I WAS STARTIN' TO DEVELOP A HAIRBALL!
HEY, IF YOU CAN TURN ANYTHING INTO ANYTHING, WHY DON'T YOU JUST TURN A CAN OF TUNA FISH INTO DONKEY-OGRE STEW?
BECAUSE IT WOULD STILL TASTE LIKE TUNA FISH! AND I HATE TUNA FISH! NOW, BE QUIET!

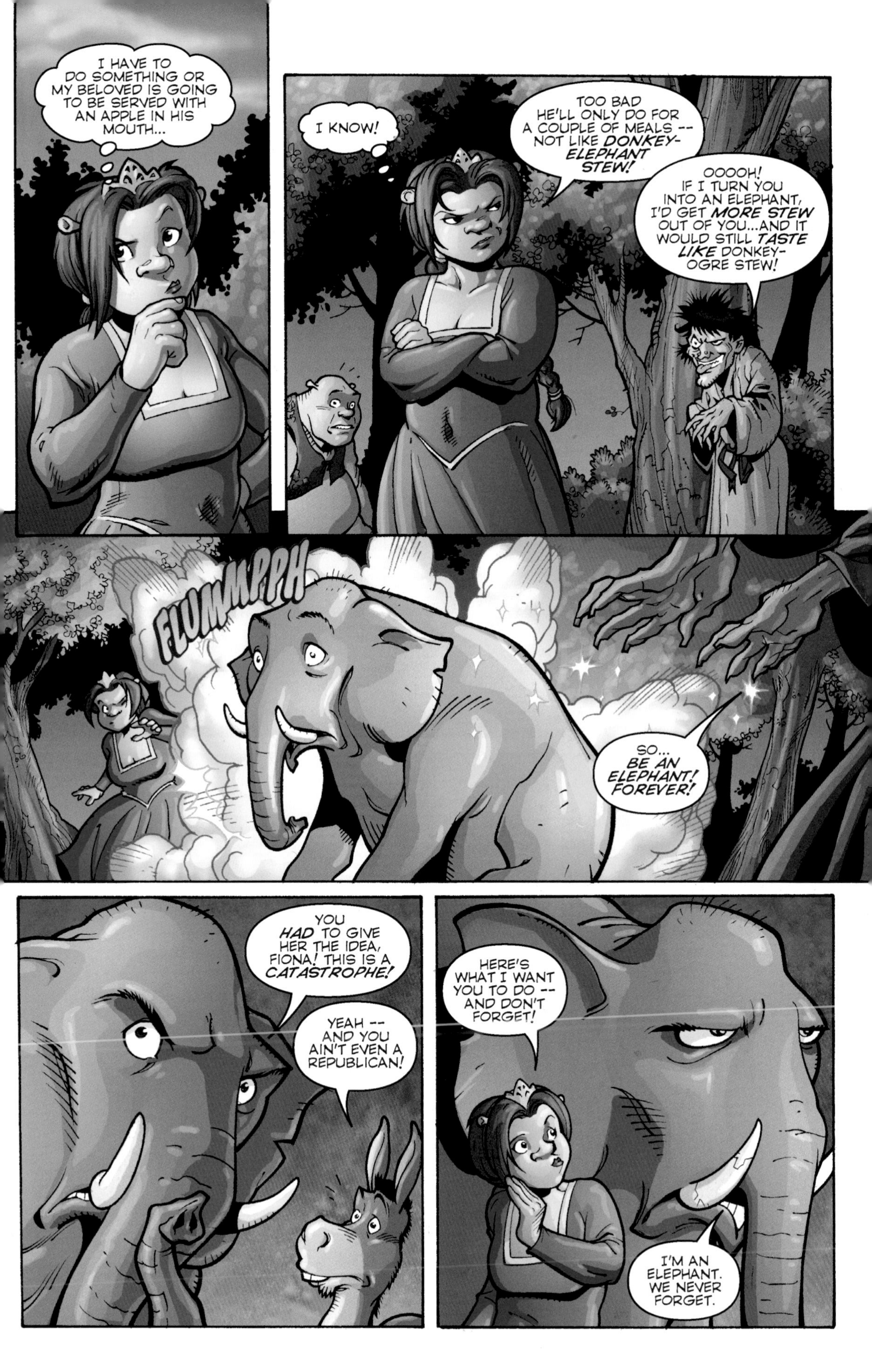
I HAVE TO DO SOMETHING OR MY BELOVED IS GOING TO BE SERVED WITH AN APPLE IN HIS MOUTH...
I KNOW!
TOO BAD HE'LL ONLY DO FOR A COUPLE OF MEALS -- NOT LIKE DONKEY-ELEPHANT STEW!
OOOOH! IF I TURN YOU INTO AN ELEPHANT, I'D GET MORE STEW OUT OF YOU...AND IT WOULD STILL TASTE LIKE DONKEY-OGRE STEW!
FLUMMPPH
SO... BE AN ELEPHANT! FOREVER!
YOU HAD TO GIVE HER THE IDEA, FIONA! THIS IS A CATASTROPHE!
YEAH -- AND YOU AIN'T EVEN A REPUBLICAN!
HERE'S WHAT I WANT YOU TO DO -- AND DON'T FORGET!
I'M AN ELEPHANT. WE NEVER FORGET.

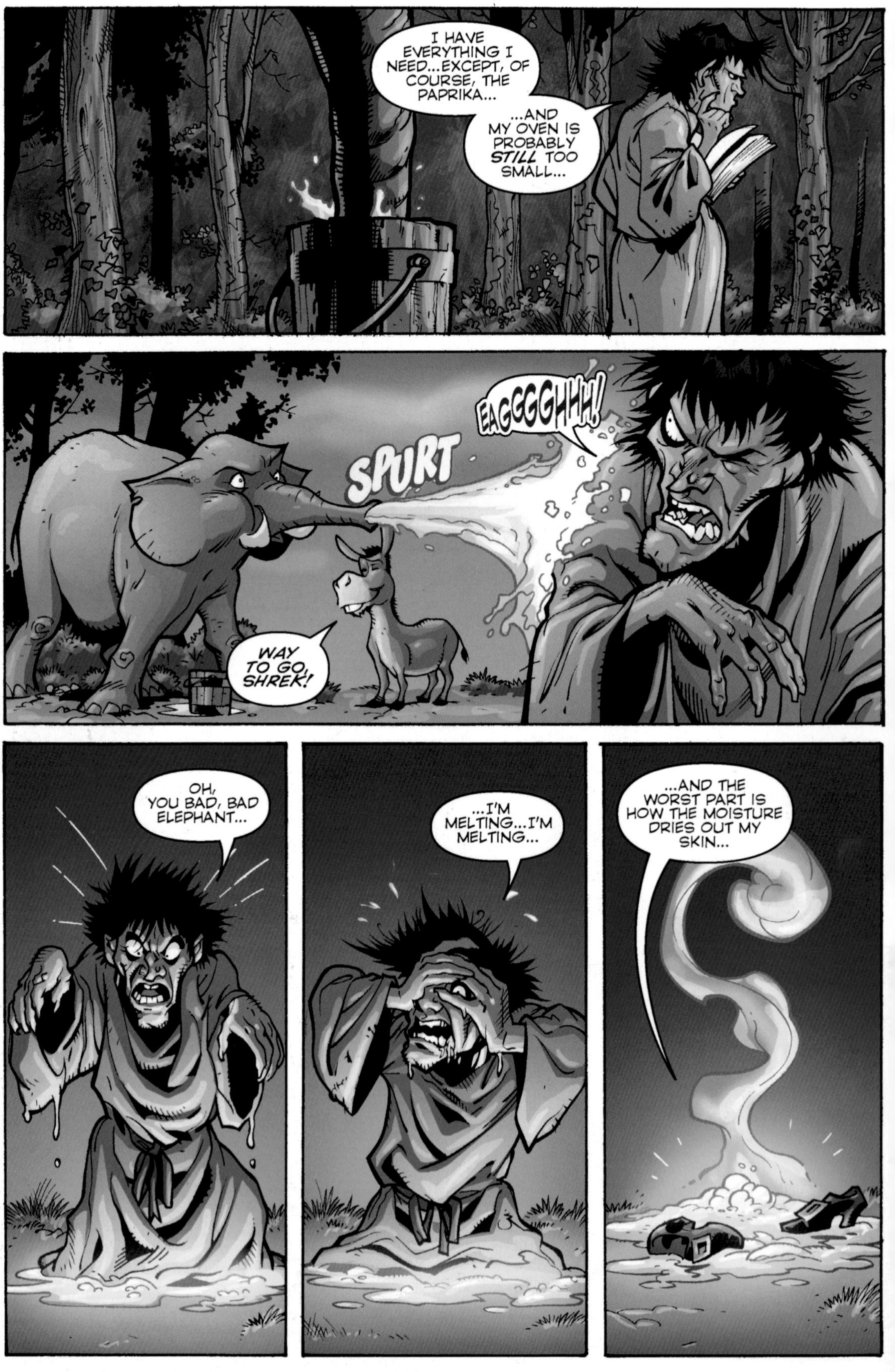
I HAVE EVERYTHING I NEED...EXCEPT, OF COURSE, THE PAPRIKA...
...AND MY OVEN IS PROBABLY STILL TOO SMALL...
SPURT
EAGGGGHHH!
WAY TO GO, SHREK!
OH, YOU BAD, BAD ELEPHANT...
...I'M MELTING...I'M MELTING...
...AND THE WORST PART IS HOW THE MOISTURE DRIES OUT MY SKIN...

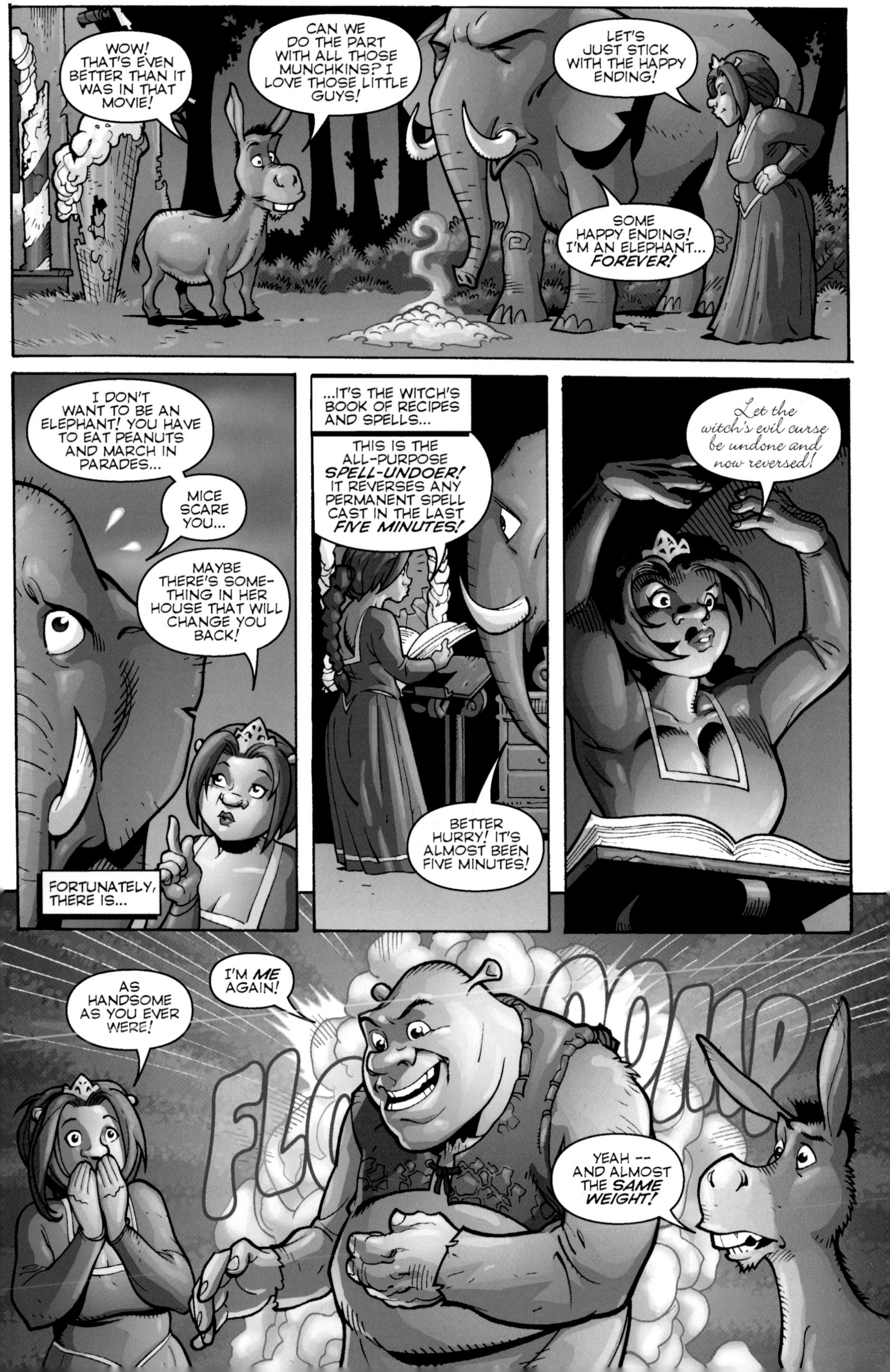
WOW! THAT'S EVEN BETTER THAN IT WAS IN THAT MOVIE!
CAN WE DO THE PART WITH ALL THOSE MUNCHKINS? I LOVE THOSE LITTLE GUYS!
LET'S JUST STICK WITH THE HAPPY ENDING!
SOME HAPPY ENDING! I'M AN ELEPHANT... FOREVER!
I DON'T WANT TO BE AN ELEPHANT! YOU HAVE TO EAT PEANUTS AND MARCH IN PARADES...
MICE SCARE YOU...
MAYBE THERE'S SOMETHING IN HER HOUSE THAT WILL CHANGE YOU BACK!
FORTUNATELY, THERE IS...
...IT'S THE WITCH'S BOOK OF RECIPES AND SPELLS...
THIS IS THE ALL-PURPOSE SPELL-UNDOER! IT REVERSES ANY PERMANENT SPELL CAST IN THE LAST FIVE MINUTES!
BETTER HURRY! IT'S ALMOST BEEN FIVE MINUTES!
Let the witch's evil curse be undone and now reversed!
AS HANDSOME AS YOU EVER WERE!
I'M ME AGAIN!
YEAH -- AND ALMOST THE SAME WEIGHT!

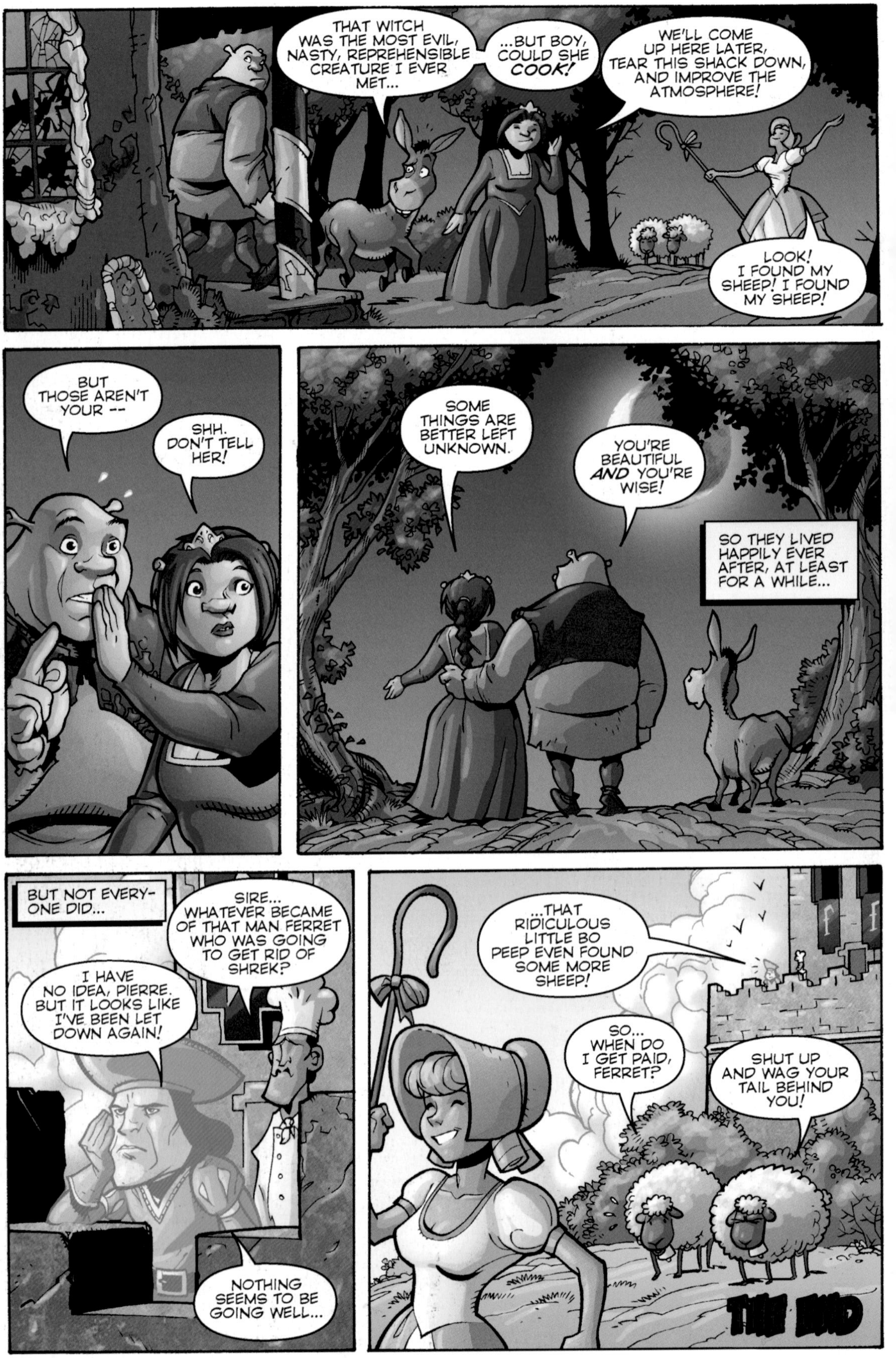

THAT WITCH WAS THE MOST EVIL, NASTY, REPREHENSIBLE CREATURE I EVER MET...
...BUT BOY, COULD SHE *COOK!*
WE'LL COME UP HERE LATER, TEAR THIS SHACK DOWN, AND IMPROVE THE ATMOSPHERE!
LOOK! I FOUND MY SHEEP! I FOUND MY SHEEP!
BUT THOSE AREN'T YOUR --
SHH. DON'T TELL HER!
SOME THINGS ARE BETTER LEFT UNKNOWN.
YOU'RE BEAUTIFUL *AND* YOU'RE WISE!
SO THEY LIVED HAPPILY EVER AFTER, AT LEAST FOR A WHILE...
BUT NOT EVERY-ONE DID...
SIRE... WHATEVER BECAME OF THAT MAN FERRET WHO WAS GOING TO GET RID OF SHREK?
I HAVE NO IDEA, PIERRE. BUT IT LOOKS LIKE I'VE BEEN LET DOWN AGAIN!
NOTHING SEEMS TO BE GOING WELL...
...THAT RIDICULOUS LITTLE BO PEEP EVEN FOUND SOME MORE SHEEP!
SO... WHEN DO I GET PAID, FERRET?
SHUT UP AND WAG YOUR TAIL BEHIND YOU!
THE END

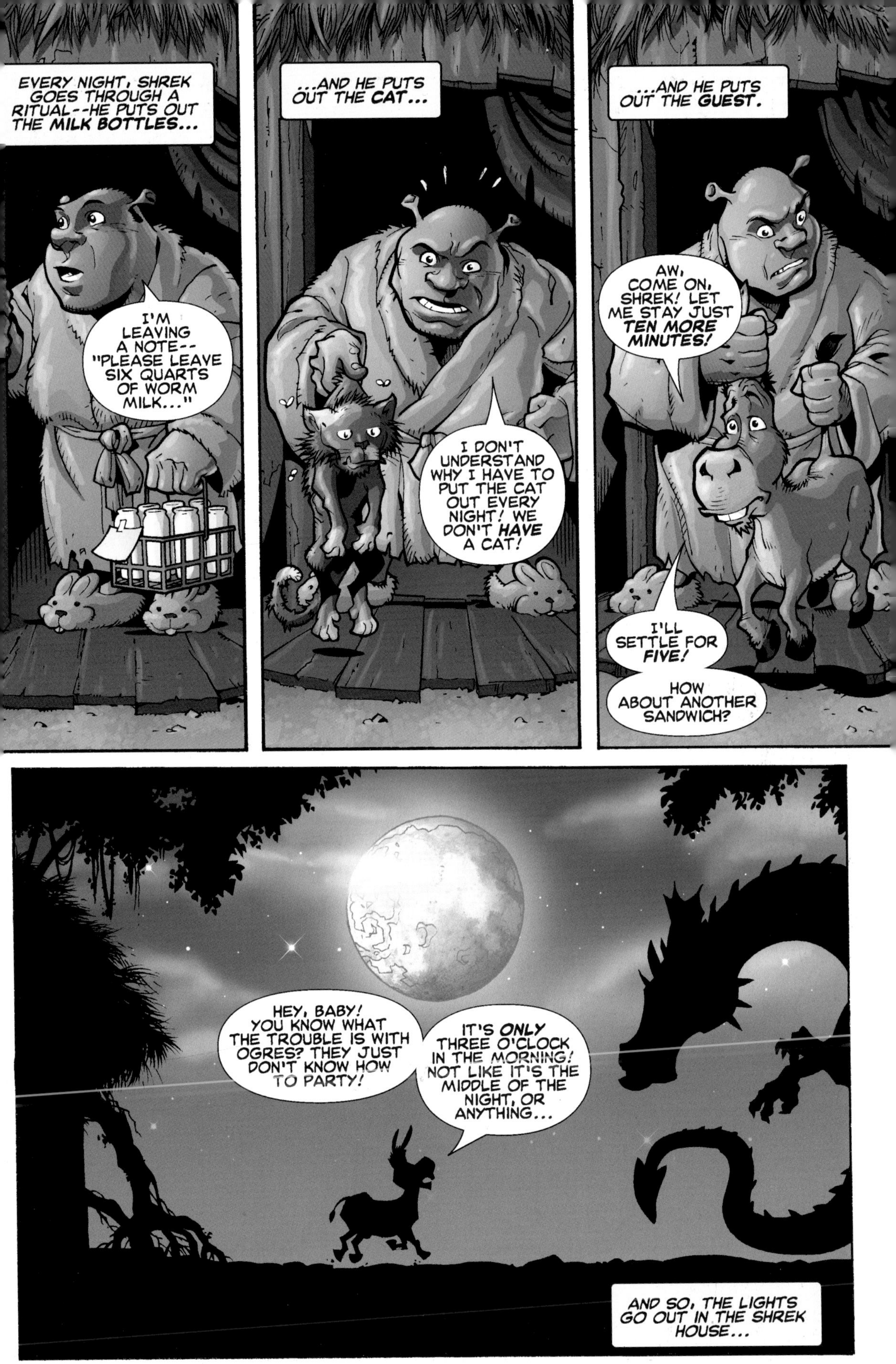
EVERY NIGHT, SHREK GOES THROUGH A RITUAL--HE PUTS OUT THE MILK BOTTLES...
I'M LEAVING A NOTE--"PLEASE LEAVE SIX QUARTS OF WORM MILK..."
...AND HE PUTS OUT THE CAT...
I DON'T UNDERSTAND WHY I HAVE TO PUT THE CAT OUT EVERY NIGHT! WE DON'T HAVE A CAT!
...AND HE PUTS OUT THE GUEST.
AW, COME ON, SHREK! LET ME STAY JUST TEN MORE MINUTES!
I'LL SETTLE FOR FIVE!
HOW ABOUT ANOTHER SANDWICH?
HEY, BABY! YOU KNOW WHAT THE TROUBLE IS WITH OGRES? THEY JUST DON'T KNOW HOW TO PARTY!
IT'S ONLY THREE O'CLOCK IN THE MORNING! NOT LIKE IT'S THE MIDDLE OF THE NIGHT, OR ANYTHING...
AND SO, THE LIGHTS GO OUT IN THE SHREK HOUSE...

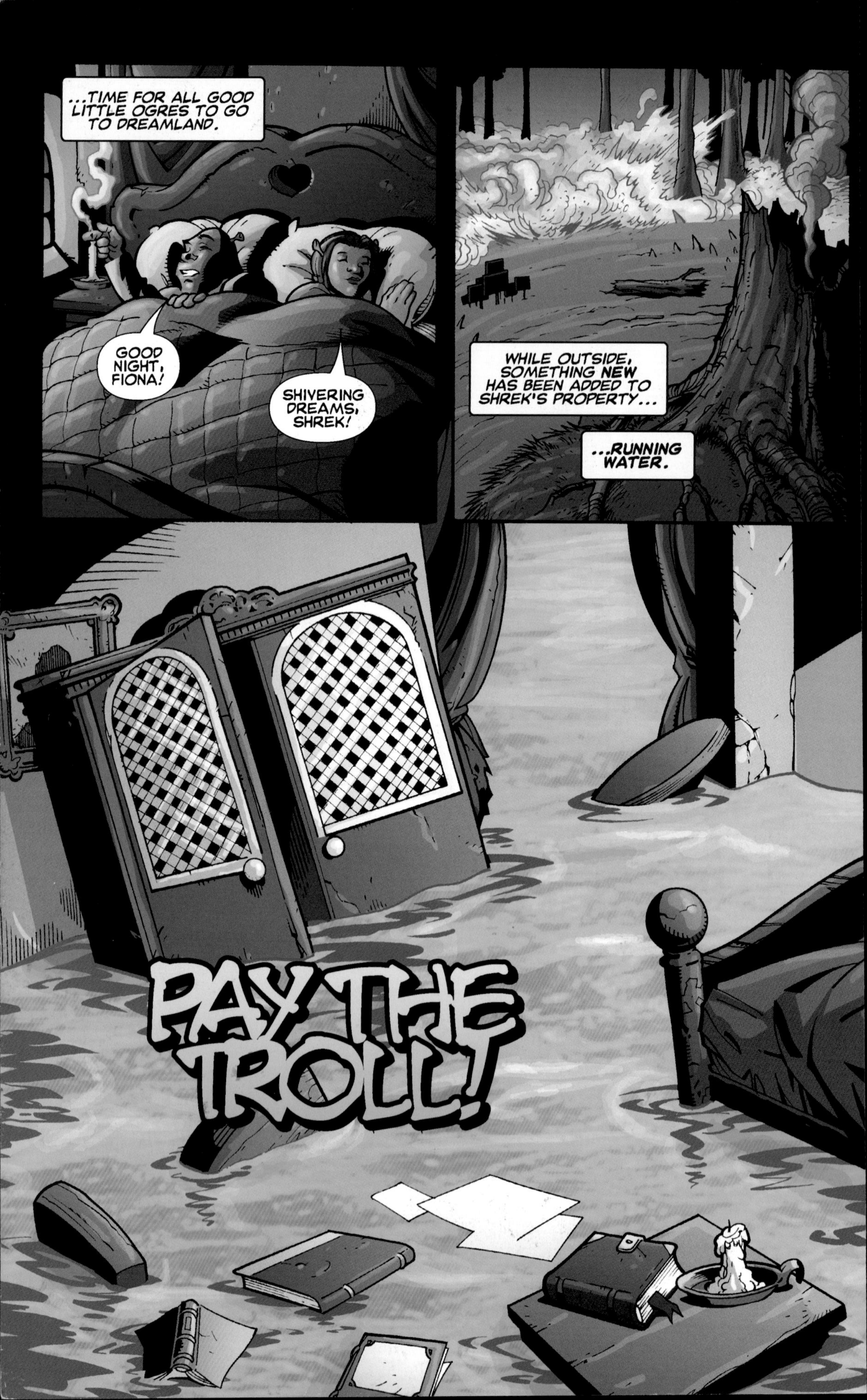
...TIME FOR ALL GOOD LITTLE OGRES TO GO TO DREAMLAND.
GOOD NIGHT, FIONA!
SHIVERING DREAMS, SHREK!
WHILE OUTSIDE, SOMETHING NEW HAS BEEN ADDED TO SHREK'S PROPERTY...
...RUNNING WATER.
PAY THE TROLL!

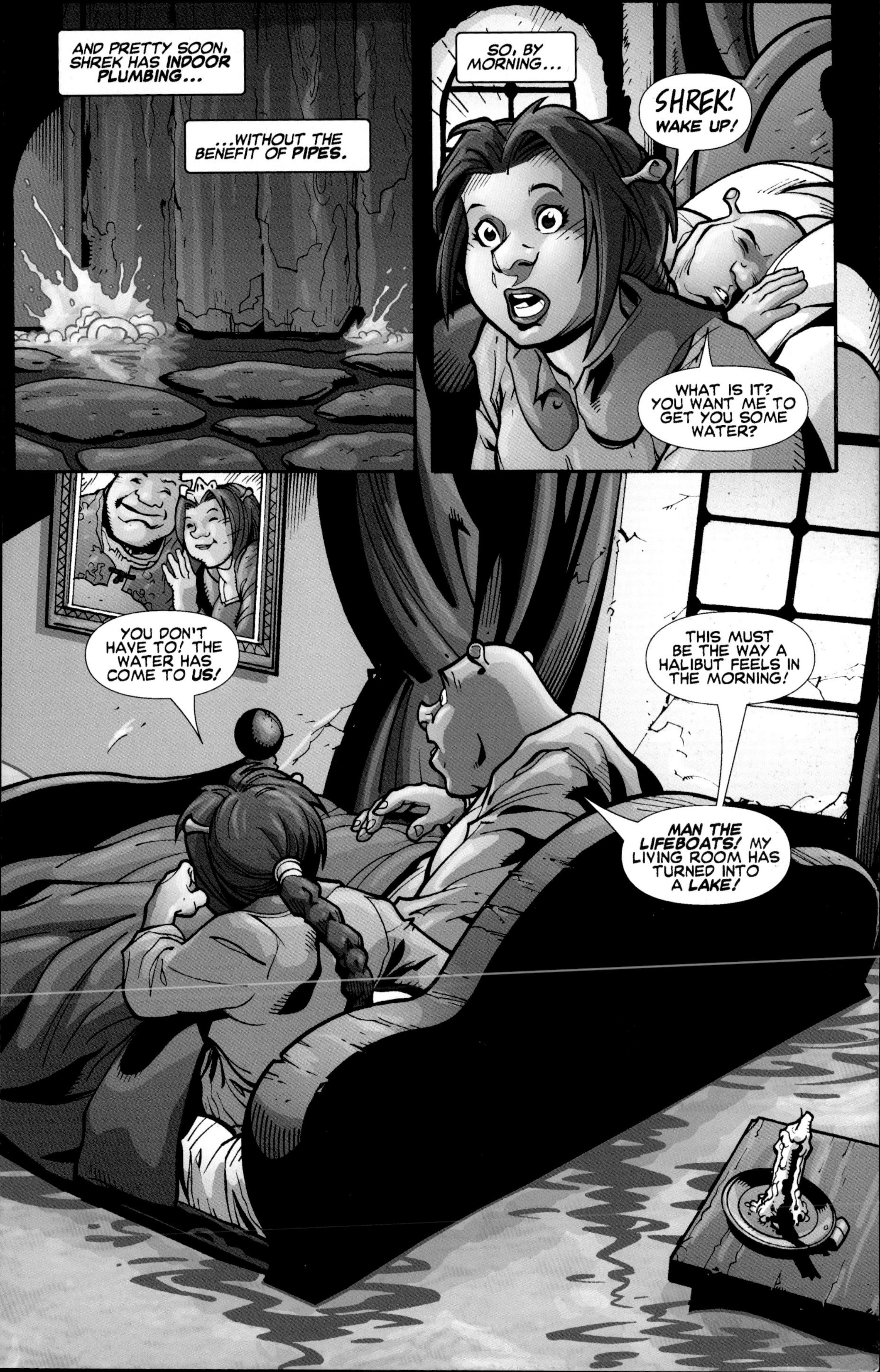
AND PRETTY SOON, SHREK HAS INDOOR PLUMBING...
...WITHOUT THE BENEFIT OF PIPES.
SO, BY MORNING...
SHREK! WAKE UP!
WHAT IS IT? YOU WANT ME TO GET YOU SOME WATER?
YOU DON'T HAVE TO! THE WATER HAS COME TO US!
THIS MUST BE THE WAY A HALIBUT FEELS IN THE MORNING!
MAN THE LIFEBOATS! MY LIVING ROOM HAS TURNED INTO A LAKE!

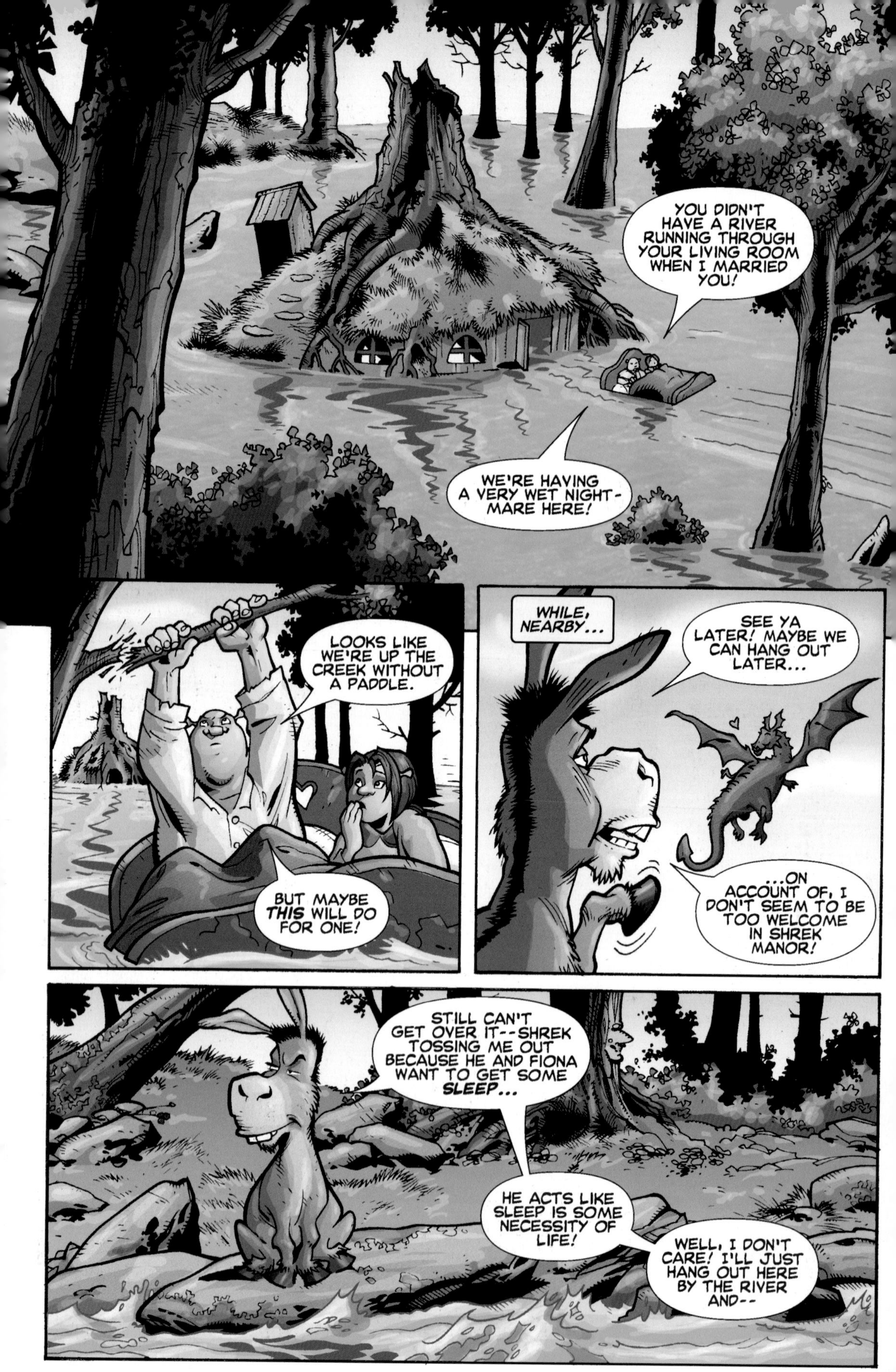
YOU DIDN'T HAVE A RIVER RUNNING THROUGH YOUR LIVING ROOM WHEN I MARRIED YOU!
WE'RE HAVING A VERY WET NIGHT-MARE HERE!
LOOKS LIKE WE'RE UP THE CREEK WITHOUT A PADDLE.
BUT MAYBE THIS WILL DO FOR ONE!
WHILE, NEARBY...
SEE YA LATER! MAYBE WE CAN HANG OUT LATER...
...ON ACCOUNT OF, I DON'T SEEM TO BE TOO WELCOME IN SHREK MANOR!
STILL CAN'T GET OVER IT--SHREK TOSSING ME OUT BECAUSE HE AND FIONA WANT TO GET SOME SLEEP...
HE ACTS LIKE SLEEP IS SOME NECESSITY OF LIFE!
WELL, I DON'T CARE! I'LL JUST HANG OUT HERE BY THE RIVER AND--

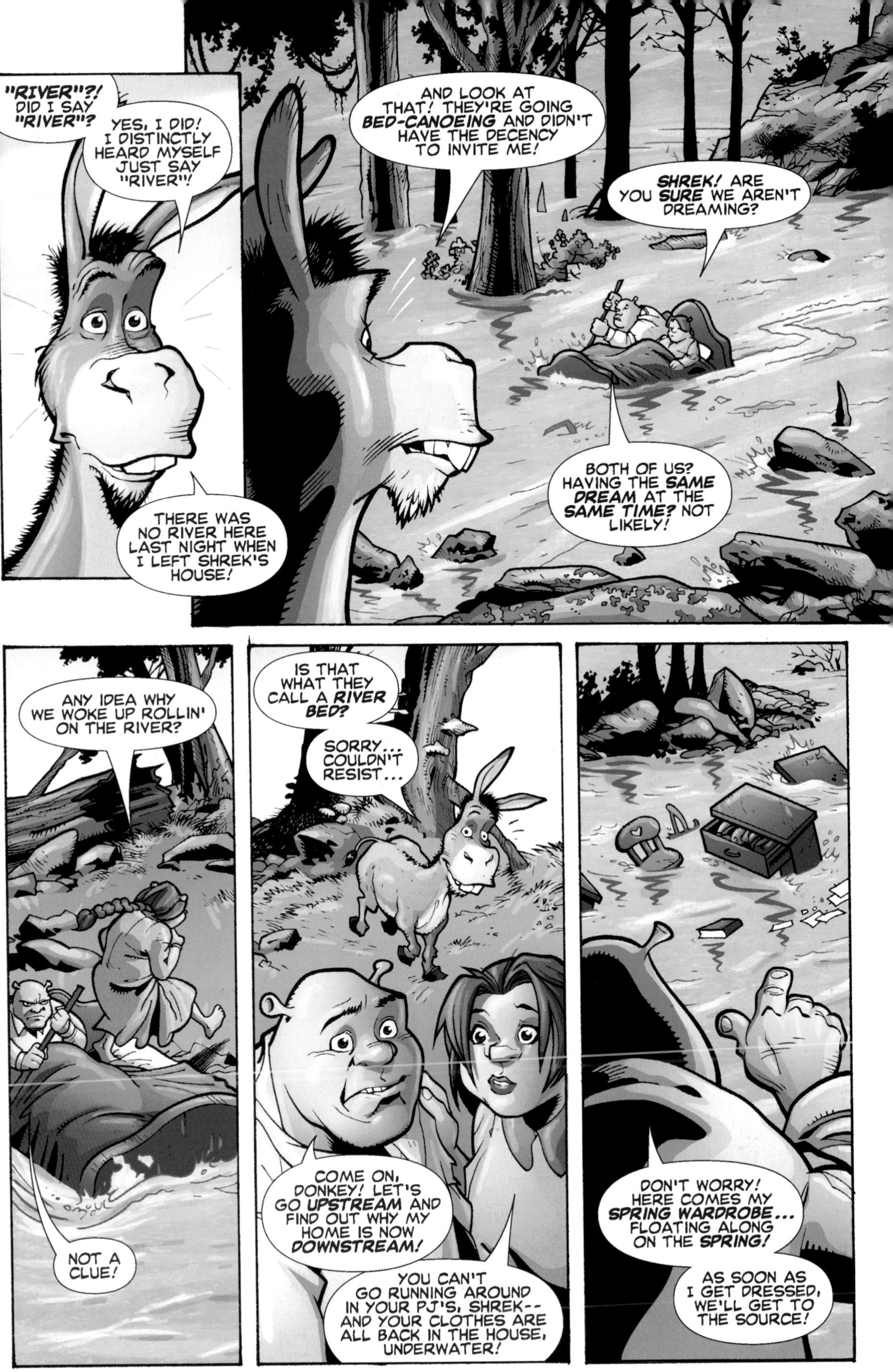
"RIVER"?! DID I SAY "RIVER"?
YES, I DID! I DISTINCTLY HEARD MYSELF JUST SAY "RIVER"!
THERE WAS NO RIVER HERE LAST NIGHT WHEN I LEFT SHREK'S HOUSE!
AND LOOK AT THAT! THEY'RE GOING BED-CANOEING AND DIDN'T HAVE THE DECENCY TO INVITE ME!
SHREK! ARE YOU SURE WE AREN'T DREAMING?
BOTH OF US? HAVING THE SAME DREAM AT THE SAME TIME? NOT LIKELY!
ANY IDEA WHY WE WOKE UP ROLLIN' ON THE RIVER?
NOT A CLUE!
IS THAT WHAT THEY CALL A RIVER BED?
SORRY... COULDN'T RESIST...
COME ON, DONKEY! LET'S GO UPSTREAM AND FIND OUT WHY MY HOME IS NOW DOWNSTREAM!
YOU CAN'T GO RUNNING AROUND IN YOUR PJ'S, SHREK-- AND YOUR CLOTHES ARE ALL BACK IN THE HOUSE, UNDERWATER!
DON'T WORRY! HERE COMES MY SPRING WARDROBE... FLOATING ALONG ON THE SPRING!
AS SOON AS I GET DRESSED, WE'LL GET TO THE SOURCE!

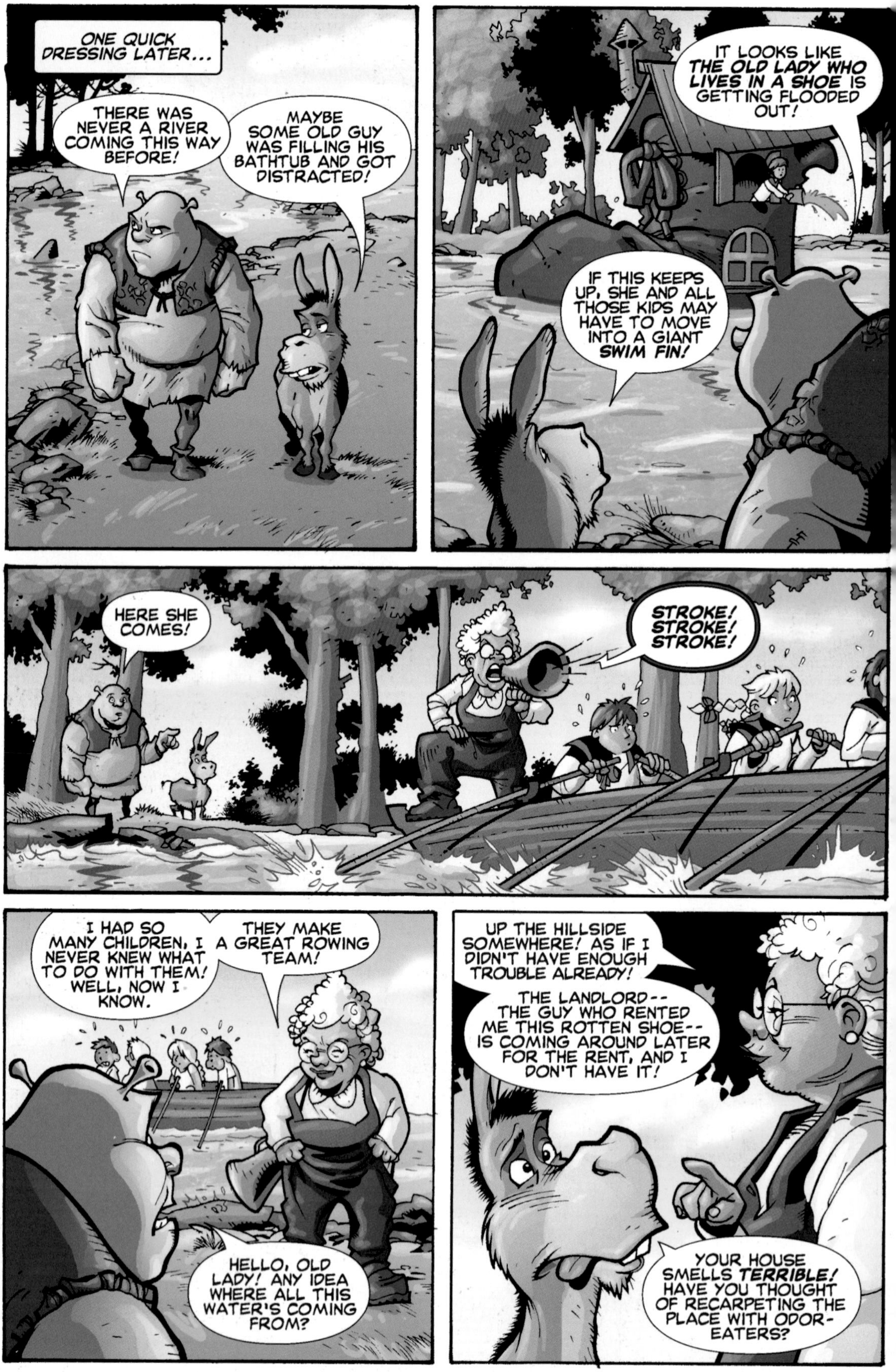
ONE QUICK DRESSING LATER...
THERE WAS NEVER A RIVER COMING THIS WAY BEFORE!
MAYBE SOME OLD GUY WAS FILLING HIS BATHTUB AND GOT DISTRACTED!
IT LOOKS LIKE THE OLD LADY WHO LIVES IN A SHOE IS GETTING FLOODED OUT!
IF THIS KEEPS UP, SHE AND ALL THOSE KIDS MAY HAVE TO MOVE INTO A GIANT SWIM FIN!
HERE SHE COMES!
STROKE! STROKE! STROKE!
I HAD SO MANY CHILDREN, I NEVER KNEW WHAT TO DO WITH THEM! WELL, NOW I KNOW.
THEY MAKE A GREAT ROWING TEAM!
HELLO, OLD LADY! ANY IDEA WHERE ALL THIS WATER'S COMING FROM?
UP THE HILLSIDE SOMEWHERE! AS IF I DIDN'T HAVE ENOUGH TROUBLE ALREADY!
THE LANDLORD-- THE GUY WHO RENTED ME THIS ROTTEN SHOE-- IS COMING AROUND LATER FOR THE RENT, AND I DON'T HAVE IT!
YOUR HOUSE SMELLS TERRIBLE! HAVE YOU THOUGHT OF RECARPETING THE PLACE WITH ODOR-EATERS?

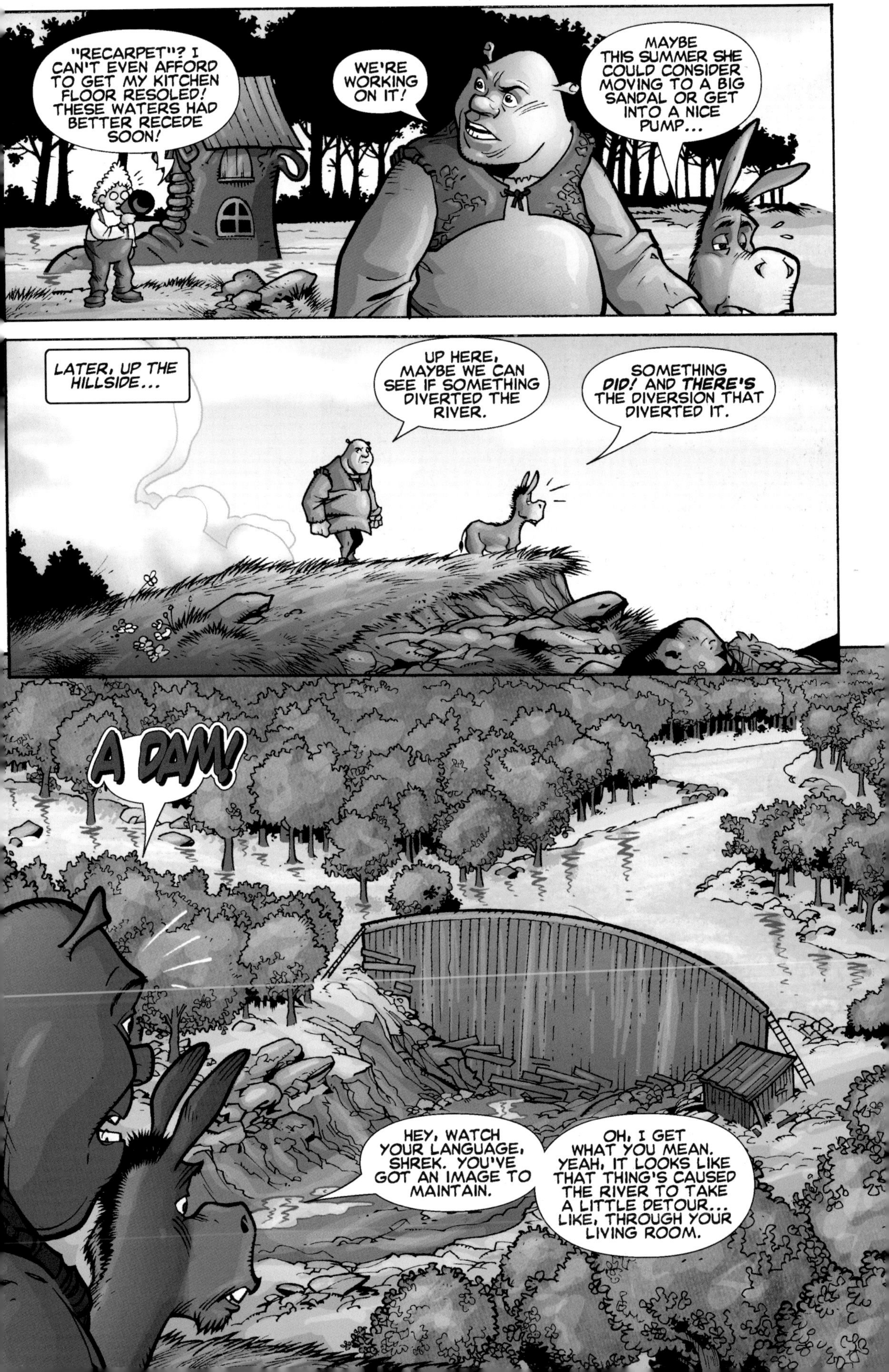
"RECARPET"? I CAN'T EVEN AFFORD TO GET MY KITCHEN FLOOR RESOLED! THESE WATERS HAD BETTER RECEDE SOON!
WE'RE WORKING ON IT!
MAYBE THIS SUMMER SHE COULD CONSIDER MOVING TO A BIG SANDAL OR GET INTO A NICE PUMP...
LATER, UP THE HILLSIDE...
UP HERE, MAYBE WE CAN SEE IF SOMETHING DIVERTED THE RIVER.
SOMETHING DID! AND THERE'S THE DIVERSION THAT DIVERTED IT.
A DAM!
HEY, WATCH YOUR LANGUAGE, SHREK. YOU'VE GOT AN IMAGE TO MAINTAIN.
OH, I GET WHAT YOU MEAN. YEAH, IT LOOKS LIKE THAT THING'S CAUSED THE RIVER TO TAKE A LITTLE DETOUR... LIKE, THROUGH YOUR LIVING ROOM.

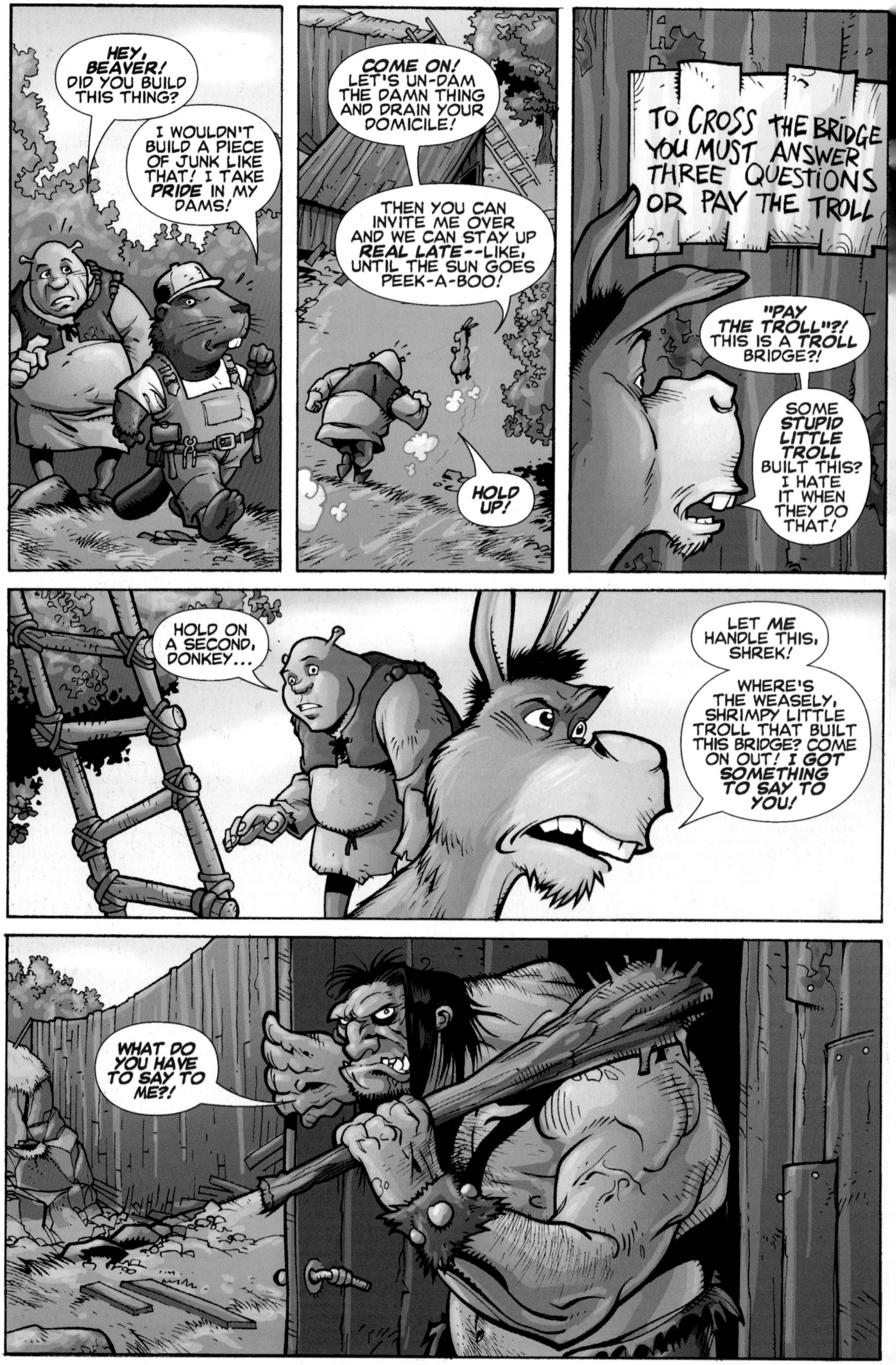

HEY, BEAVER! DID YOU BUILD THIS THING?
I WOULDN'T BUILD A PIECE OF JUNK LIKE THAT! I TAKE PRIDE IN MY DAMS!
COME ON! LET'S UN-DAM THE DAMN THING AND DRAIN YOUR DOMICILE!
THEN YOU CAN INVITE ME OVER AND WE CAN STAY UP REAL LATE--LIKE, UNTIL THE SUN GOES PEEK-A-BOO!
HOLD UP!
TO CROSS THE BRIDGE YOU MUST ANSWER THREE QUESTIONS OR PAY THE TROLL
"PAY THE TROLL"?! THIS IS A TROLL BRIDGE?!
SOME STUPID LITTLE TROLL BUILT THIS? I HATE IT WHEN THEY DO THAT!
HOLD ON A SECOND, DONKEY...
LET ME HANDLE THIS, SHREK!
WHERE'S THE WEASELY, SHRIMPY LITTLE TROLL THAT BUILT THIS BRIDGE? COME ON OUT! I GOT SOMETHING TO SAY TO YOU!
WHAT DO YOU HAVE TO SAY TO ME?!

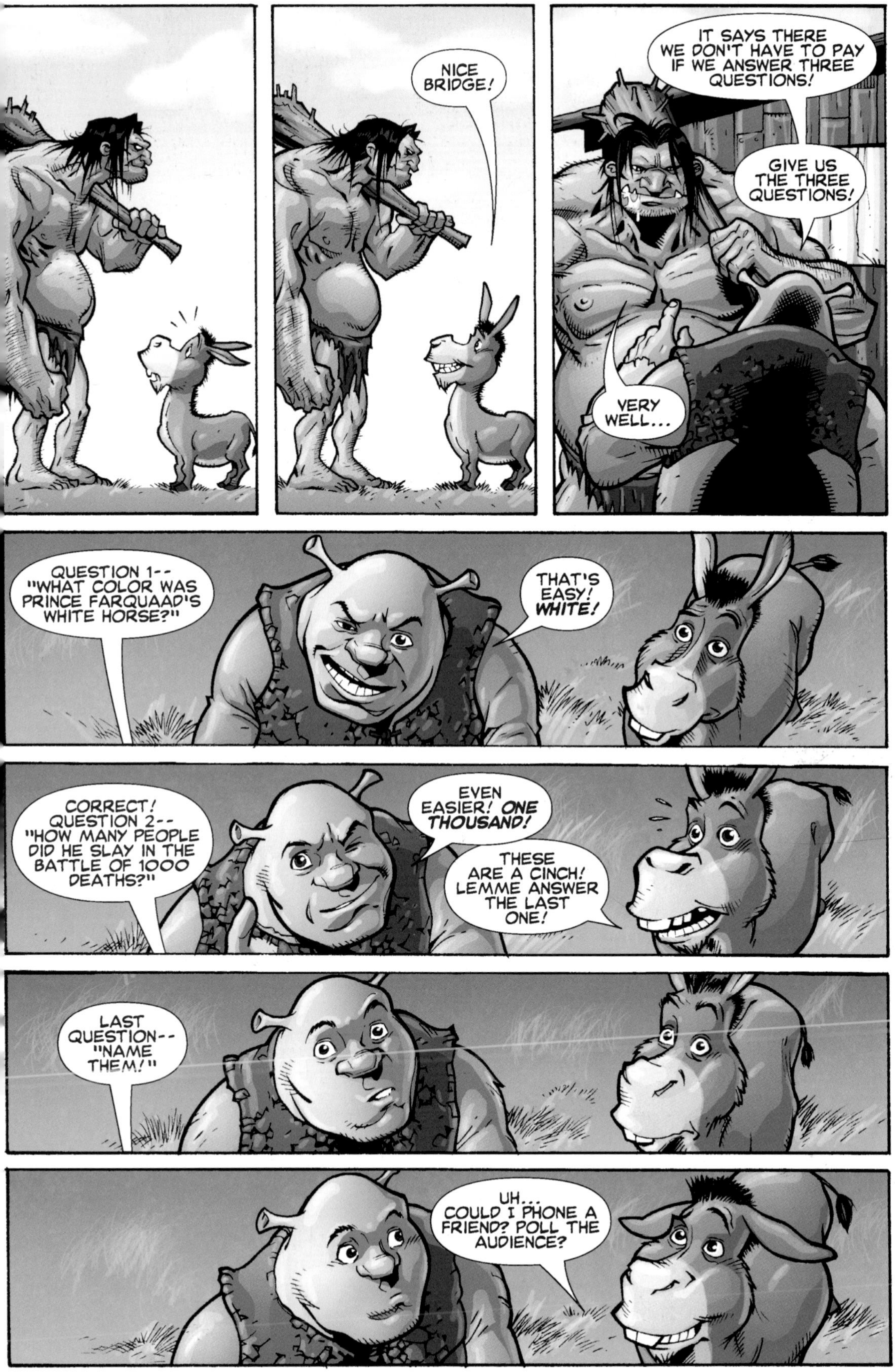
NICE BRIDGE!
IT SAYS THERE WE DON'T HAVE TO PAY IF WE ANSWER THREE QUESTIONS!
GIVE US THE THREE QUESTIONS!
VERY WELL...
QUESTION 1-- "WHAT COLOR WAS PRINCE FARQUAAD'S WHITE HORSE?"
THAT'S EASY! WHITE!
CORRECT! QUESTION 2-- "HOW MANY PEOPLE DID HE SLAY IN THE BATTLE OF 1000 DEATHS?"
EVEN EASIER! ONE THOUSAND!
THESE ARE A CINCH! LEMME ANSWER THE LAST ONE!
LAST QUESTION-- "NAME THEM!"
UH... COULD I PHONE A FRIEND? POLL THE AUDIENCE?

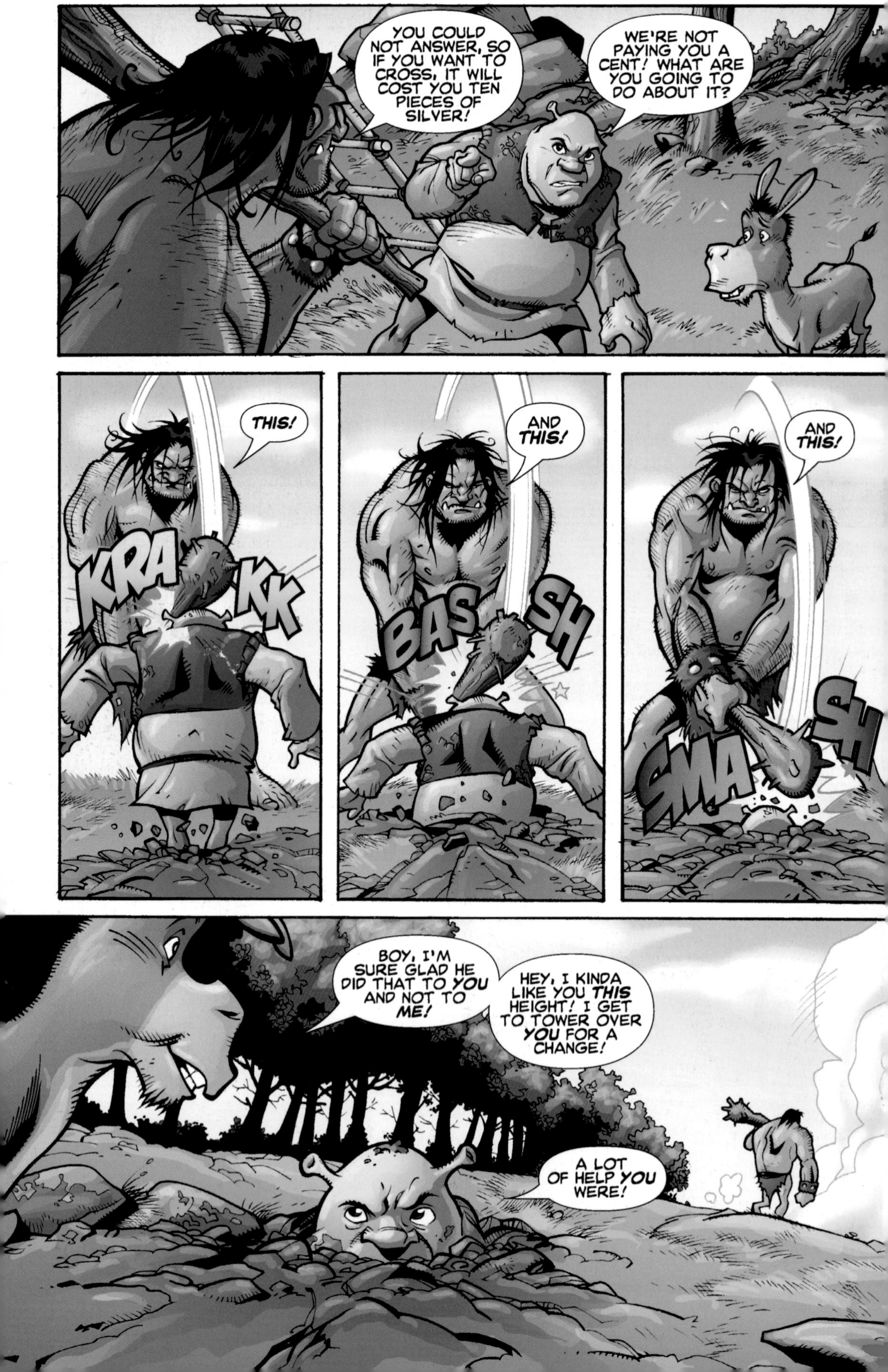
YOU COULD NOT ANSWER, SO IF YOU WANT TO CROSS, IT WILL COST YOU TEN PIECES OF SILVER!
WE'RE NOT PAYING YOU A CENT! WHAT ARE YOU GOING TO DO ABOUT IT?
THIS!
KRAKK
AND THIS!
BASSH
AND THIS!
SMASH
BOY, I'M SURE GLAD HE DID THAT TO YOU AND NOT TO ME!
HEY, I KINDA LIKE YOU THIS HEIGHT! I GET TO TOWER OVER YOU FOR A CHANGE!
A LOT OF HELP YOU WERE!

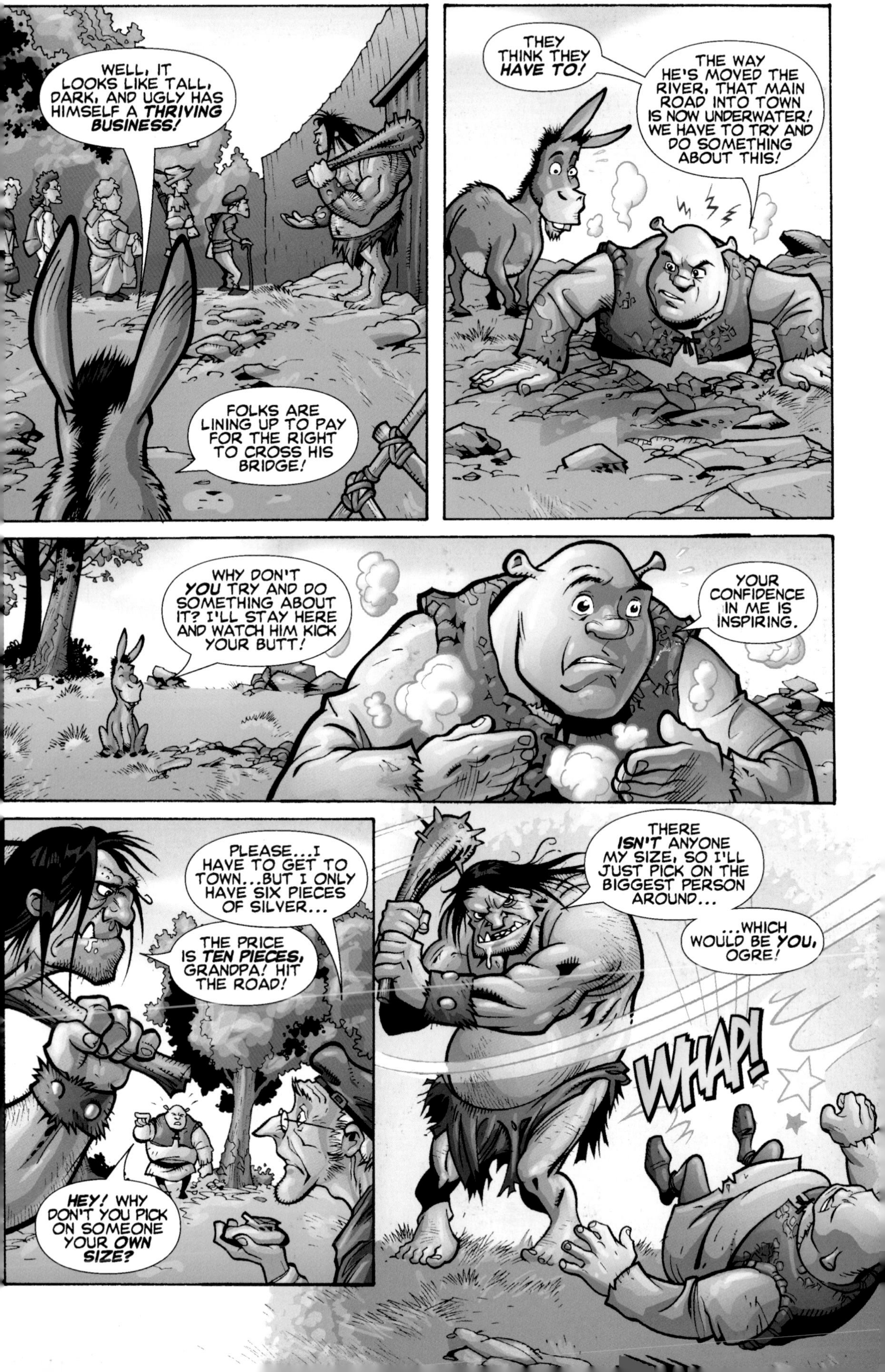

WELL, IT LOOKS LIKE TALL, DARK, AND UGLY HAS HIMSELF A THRIVING BUSINESS!
FOLKS ARE LINING UP TO PAY FOR THE RIGHT TO CROSS HIS BRIDGE!
THEY THINK THEY HAVE TO!
THE WAY HE'S MOVED THE RIVER, THAT MAIN ROAD INTO TOWN IS NOW UNDERWATER! WE HAVE TO TRY AND DO SOMETHING ABOUT THIS!
WHY DON'T YOU TRY AND DO SOMETHING ABOUT IT? I'LL STAY HERE AND WATCH HIM KICK YOUR BUTT!
YOUR CONFIDENCE IN ME IS INSPIRING.
PLEASE...I HAVE TO GET TO TOWN...BUT I ONLY HAVE SIX PIECES OF SILVER...
THE PRICE IS TEN PIECES, GRANDPA! HIT THE ROAD!
HEY! WHY DON'T YOU PICK ON SOMEONE YOUR OWN SIZE?
THERE ISN'T ANYONE MY SIZE, SO I'LL JUST PICK ON THE BIGGEST PERSON AROUND...
...WHICH WOULD BE YOU, OGRE!
WHAP!

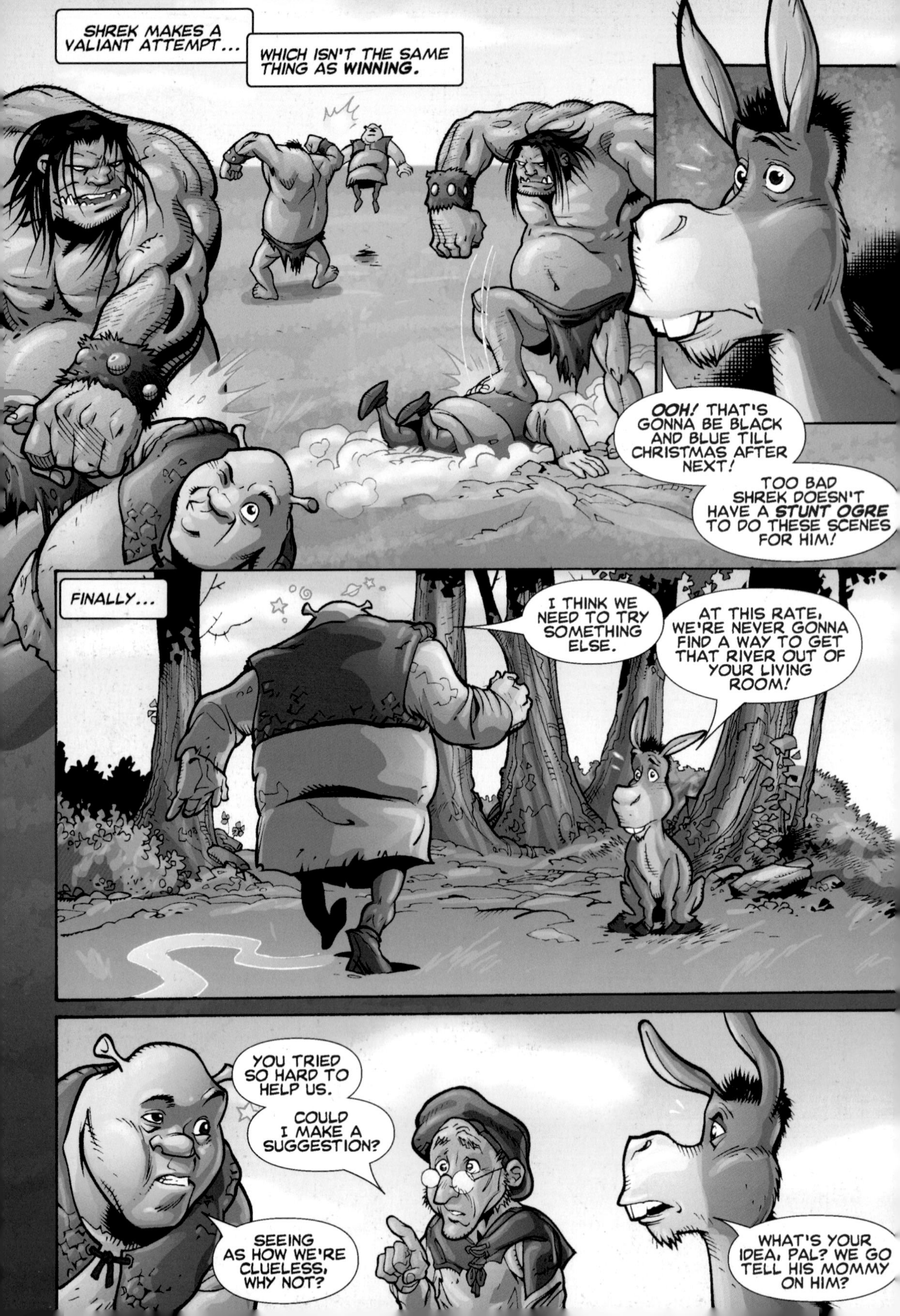
SHREK MAKES A VALIANT ATTEMPT...
WHICH ISN'T THE SAME THING AS **WINNING**.
OOH! THAT'S GONNA BE BLACK AND BLUE TILL CHRISTMAS AFTER NEXT!
TOO BAD SHREK DOESN'T HAVE A ***STUNT OGRE*** TO DO THESE SCENES FOR HIM!
FINALLY...
I THINK WE NEED TO TRY SOMETHING ELSE.
AT THIS RATE, WE'RE NEVER GONNA FIND A WAY TO GET THAT RIVER OUT OF YOUR LIVING ROOM!
YOU TRIED SO HARD TO HELP US.
COULD I MAKE A SUGGESTION?
SEEING AS HOW WE'RE CLUELESS, WHY NOT?
WHAT'S YOUR IDEA, PAL? WE GO TELL HIS MOMMY ON HIM?

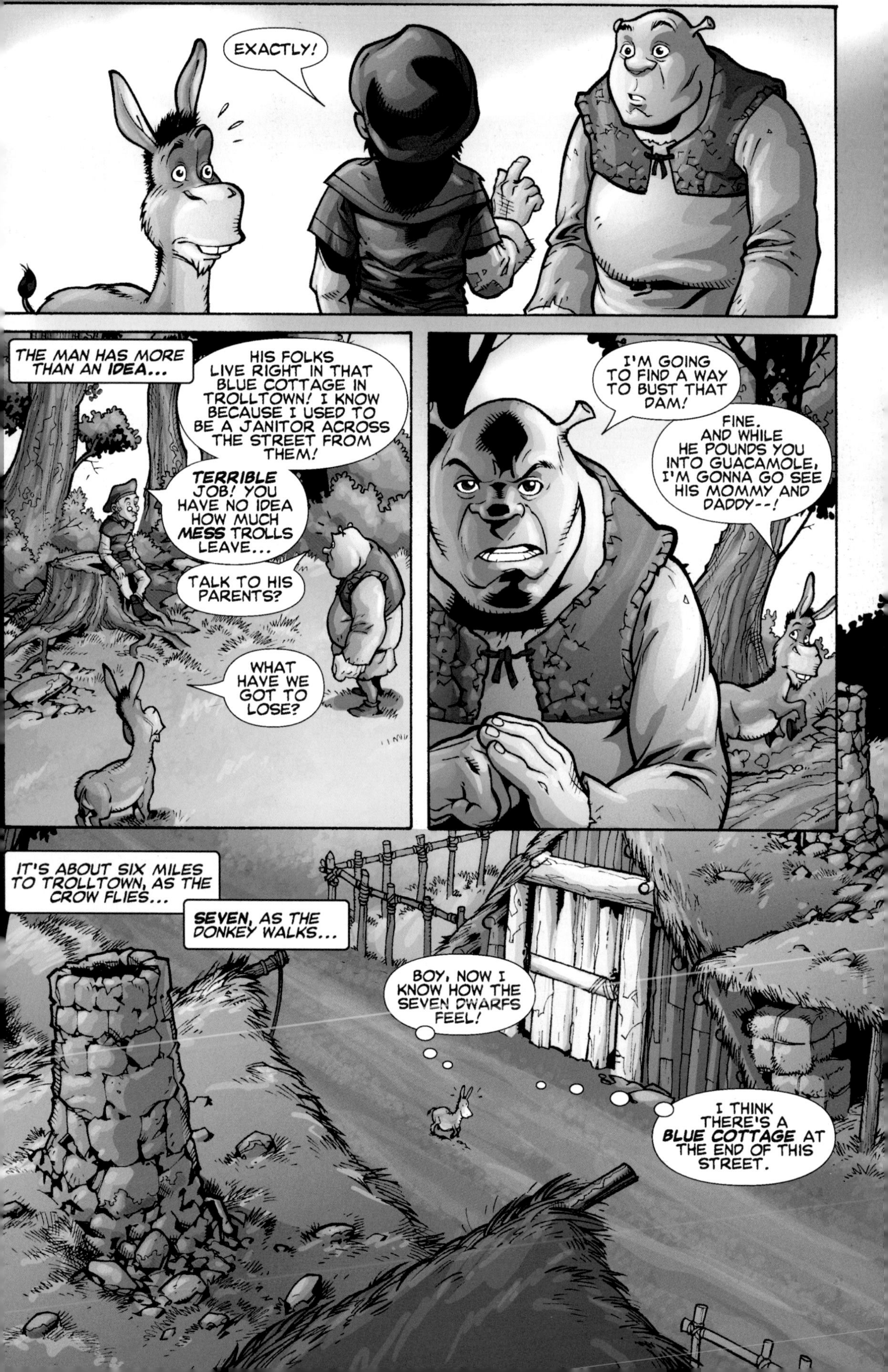
EXACTLY!
THE MAN HAS MORE THAN AN IDEA...
HIS FOLKS LIVE RIGHT IN THAT BLUE COTTAGE IN TROLLTOWN! I KNOW BECAUSE I USED TO BE A JANITOR ACROSS THE STREET FROM THEM!
TERRIBLE JOB! YOU HAVE NO IDEA HOW MUCH MESS TROLLS LEAVE...
TALK TO HIS PARENTS?
WHAT HAVE WE GOT TO LOSE?
I'M GOING TO FIND A WAY TO BUST THAT DAM!
FINE. AND WHILE HE POUNDS YOU INTO GUACAMOLE, I'M GONNA GO SEE HIS MOMMY AND DADDY--!
IT'S ABOUT SIX MILES TO TROLLTOWN, AS THE CROW FLIES...
SEVEN, AS THE DONKEY WALKS...
BOY, NOW I KNOW HOW THE SEVEN DWARFS FEEL!
I THINK THERE'S A BLUE COTTAGE AT THE END OF THIS STREET.

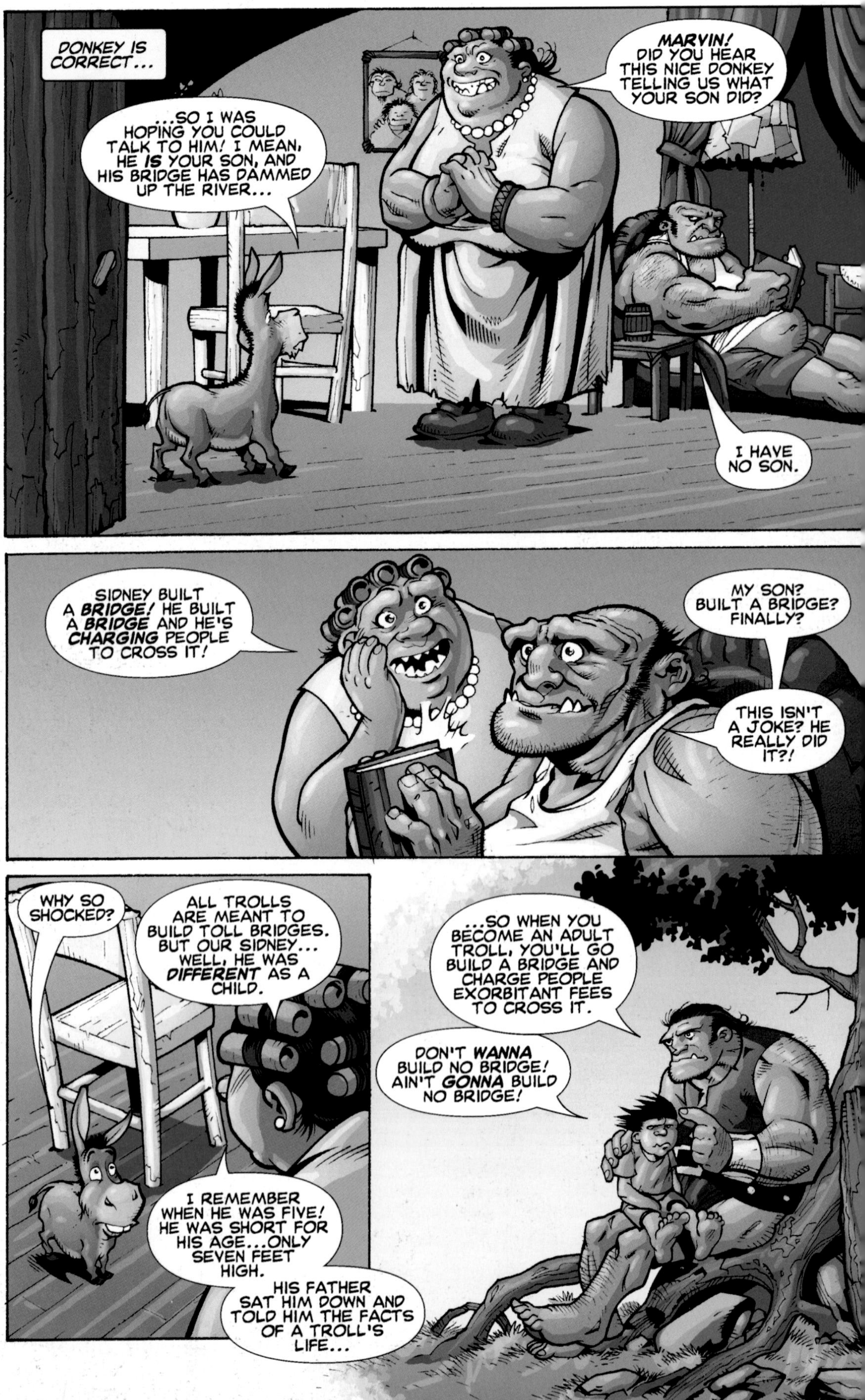
DONKEY IS CORRECT...
...SO I WAS HOPING YOU COULD TALK TO HIM! I MEAN, HE IS YOUR SON, AND HIS BRIDGE HAS DAMMED UP THE RIVER...
MARVIN! DID YOU HEAR THIS NICE DONKEY TELLING US WHAT YOUR SON DID?
I HAVE NO SON.
SIDNEY BUILT A BRIDGE! HE BUILT A BRIDGE AND HE'S CHARGING PEOPLE TO CROSS IT!
MY SON? BUILT A BRIDGE? FINALLY?
THIS ISN'T A JOKE? HE REALLY DID IT?!
WHY SO SHOCKED?
ALL TROLLS ARE MEANT TO BUILD TOLL BRIDGES. BUT OUR SIDNEY... WELL, HE WAS DIFFERENT AS A CHILD.
I REMEMBER WHEN HE WAS FIVE! HE WAS SHORT FOR HIS AGE...ONLY SEVEN FEET HIGH.
HIS FATHER SAT HIM DOWN AND TOLD HIM THE FACTS OF A TROLL'S LIFE...
...SO WHEN YOU BECOME AN ADULT TROLL, YOU'LL GO BUILD A BRIDGE AND CHARGE PEOPLE EXORBITANT FEES TO CROSS IT.
DON'T WANNA BUILD NO BRIDGE! AIN'T GONNA BUILD NO BRIDGE!

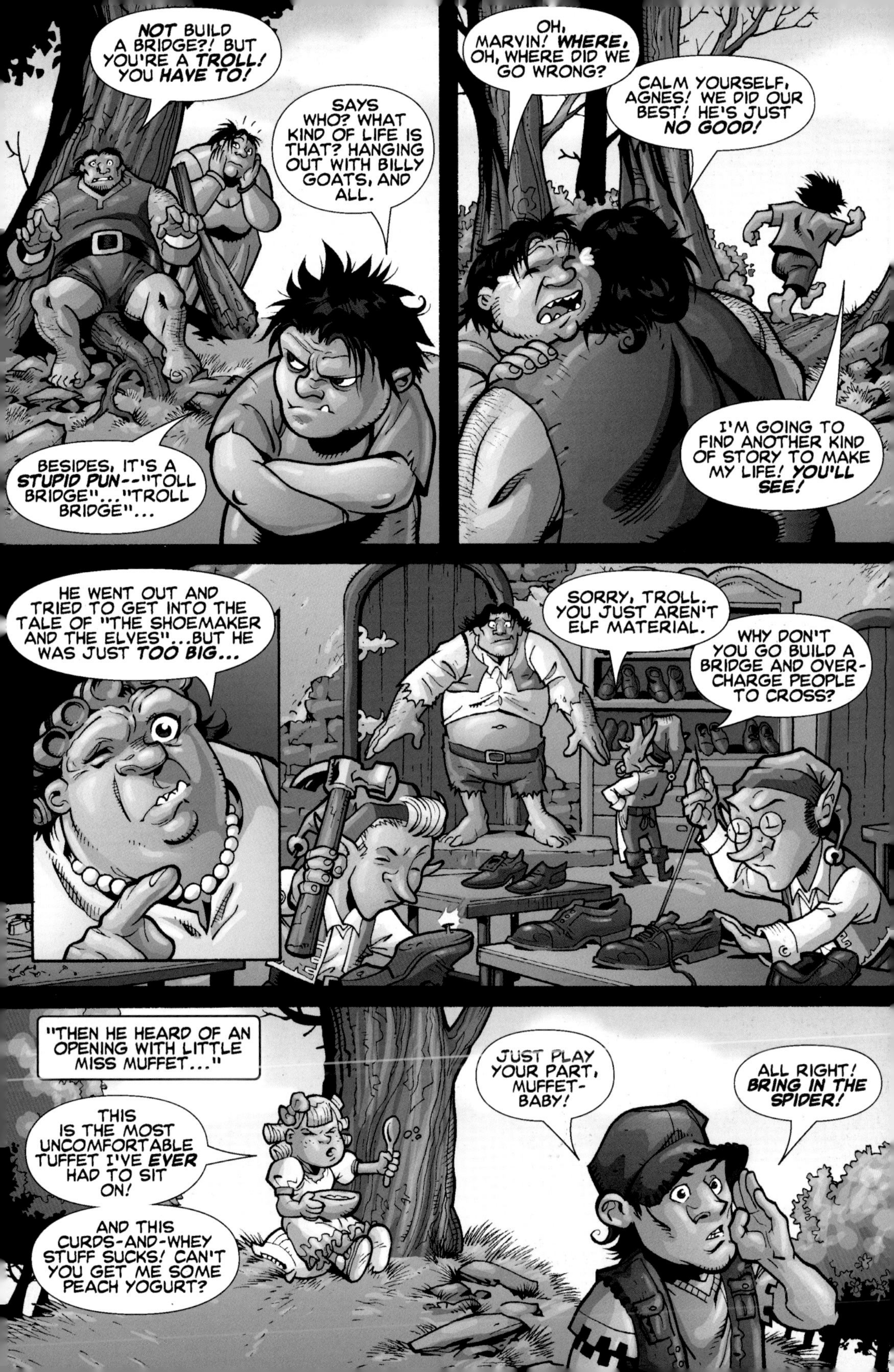
NOT BUILD A BRIDGE?! BUT YOU'RE A TROLL! YOU HAVE TO!
SAYS WHO? WHAT KIND OF LIFE IS THAT? HANGING OUT WITH BILLY GOATS, AND ALL.
BESIDES, IT'S A STUPID PUN--"TOLL BRIDGE"..."TROLL BRIDGE"...
OH, MARVIN! WHERE, OH, WHERE DID WE GO WRONG?
CALM YOURSELF, AGNES! WE DID OUR BEST! HE'S JUST NO GOOD!
I'M GOING TO FIND ANOTHER KIND OF STORY TO MAKE MY LIFE! YOU'LL SEE!
HE WENT OUT AND TRIED TO GET INTO THE TALE OF "THE SHOEMAKER AND THE ELVES"...BUT HE WAS JUST TOO BIG...
SORRY, TROLL. YOU JUST AREN'T ELF MATERIAL.
WHY DON'T YOU GO BUILD A BRIDGE AND OVER-CHARGE PEOPLE TO CROSS?
"THEN HE HEARD OF AN OPENING WITH LITTLE MISS MUFFET..."
THIS IS THE MOST UNCOMFORTABLE TUFFET I'VE EVER HAD TO SIT ON!
AND THIS CURDS-AND-WHEY STUFF SUCKS! CAN'T YOU GET ME SOME PEACH YOGURT?
JUST PLAY YOUR PART, MUFFET-BABY!
ALL RIGHT! BRING IN THE SPIDER!

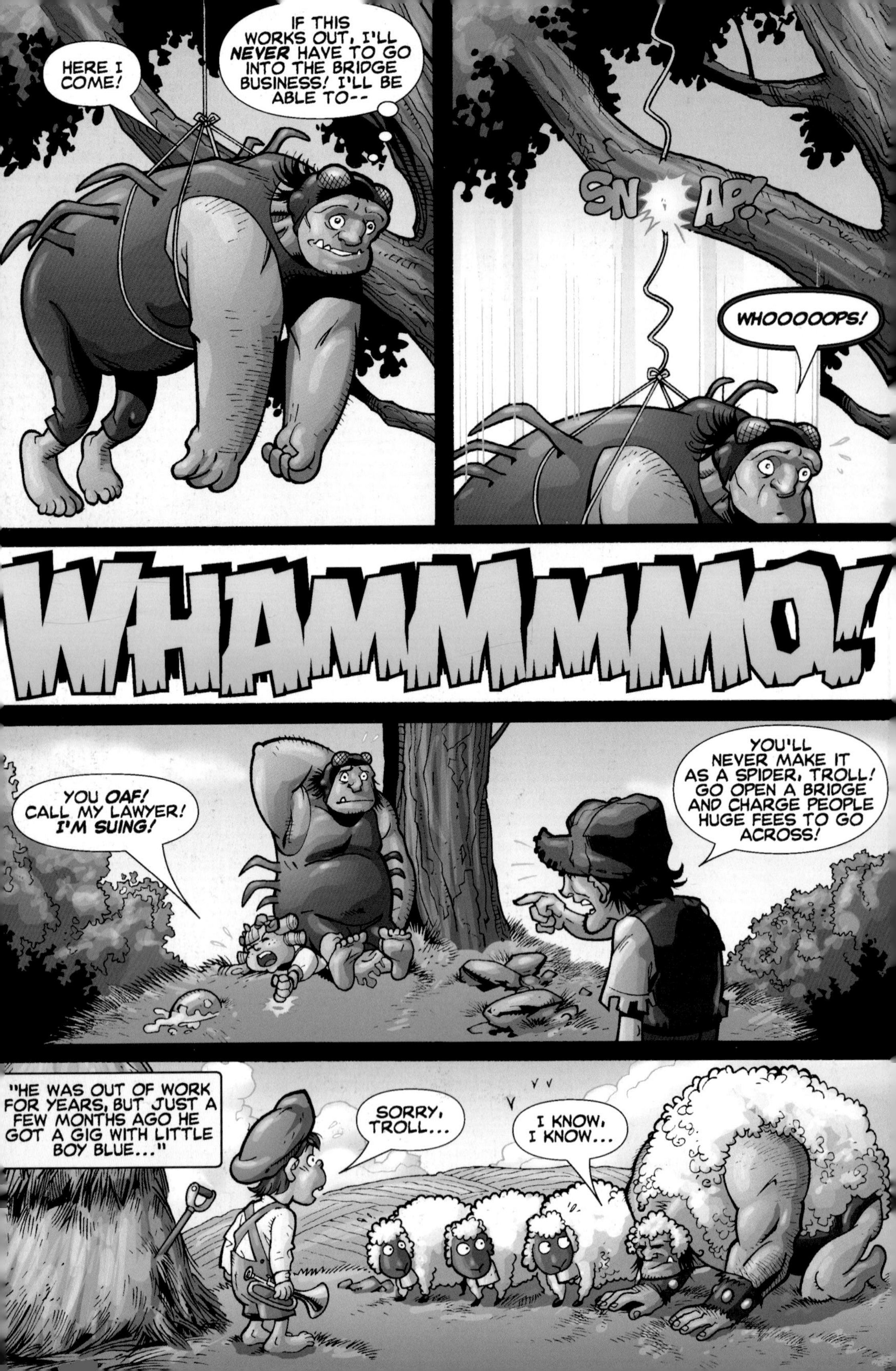
HERE I COME!
IF THIS WORKS OUT, I'LL *NEVER* HAVE TO GO INTO THE BRIDGE BUSINESS! I'LL BE ABLE TO--
SN AP!
WHOOOOOPS!
WHAMMMMMO!
YOU *OAF!* CALL MY LAWYER! *I'M SUING!*
YOU'LL NEVER MAKE IT AS A SPIDER, TROLL! GO OPEN A BRIDGE AND CHARGE PEOPLE HUGE FEES TO GO ACROSS!
"HE WAS OUT OF WORK FOR YEARS, BUT JUST A FEW MONTHS AGO HE GOT A GIG WITH LITTLE BOY BLUE..."
SORRY, TROLL...
I KNOW, I KNOW...

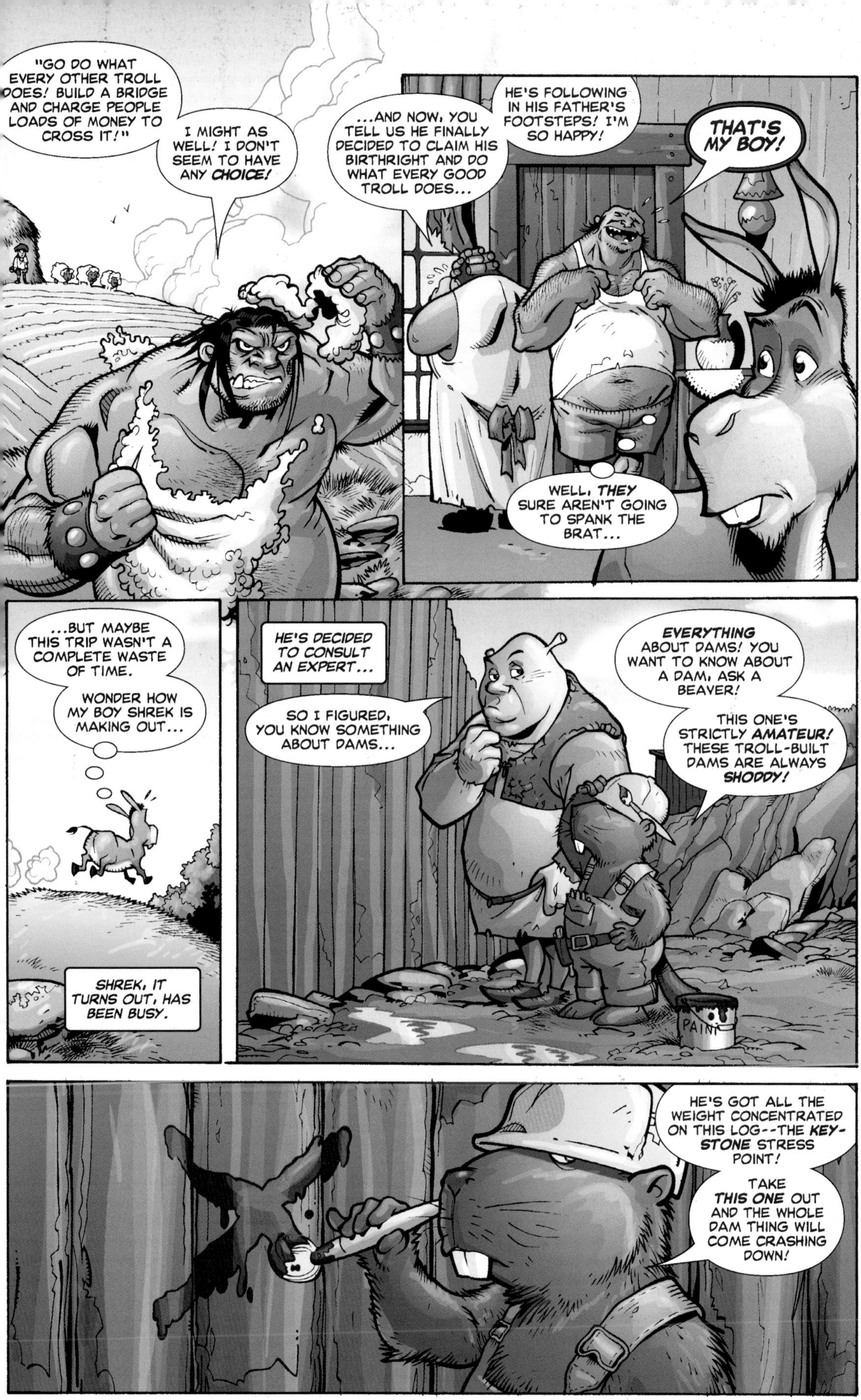
"GO DO WHAT EVERY OTHER TROLL DOES! BUILD A BRIDGE AND CHARGE PEOPLE LOADS OF MONEY TO CROSS IT!"
I MIGHT AS WELL! I DON'T SEEM TO HAVE ANY CHOICE!
...AND NOW, YOU TELL US HE FINALLY DECIDED TO CLAIM HIS BIRTHRIGHT AND DO WHAT EVERY GOOD TROLL DOES...
HE'S FOLLOWING IN HIS FATHER'S FOOTSTEPS! I'M SO HAPPY!
THAT'S MY BOY!
WELL, THEY SURE AREN'T GOING TO SPANK THE BRAT...
...BUT MAYBE THIS TRIP WASN'T A COMPLETE WASTE OF TIME.
WONDER HOW MY BOY SHREK IS MAKING OUT...
SHREK, IT TURNS OUT, HAS BEEN BUSY.
HE'S DECIDED TO CONSULT AN EXPERT...
SO I FIGURED, YOU KNOW SOMETHING ABOUT DAMS...
EVERYTHING ABOUT DAMS! YOU WANT TO KNOW ABOUT A DAM, ASK A BEAVER!
THIS ONE'S STRICTLY AMATEUR! THESE TROLL-BUILT DAMS ARE ALWAYS SHODDY!
PAINT
HE'S GOT ALL THE WEIGHT CONCENTRATED ON THIS LOG--THE KEYSTONE STRESS POINT!
TAKE THIS ONE OUT AND THE WHOLE DAM THING WILL COME CRASHING DOWN!

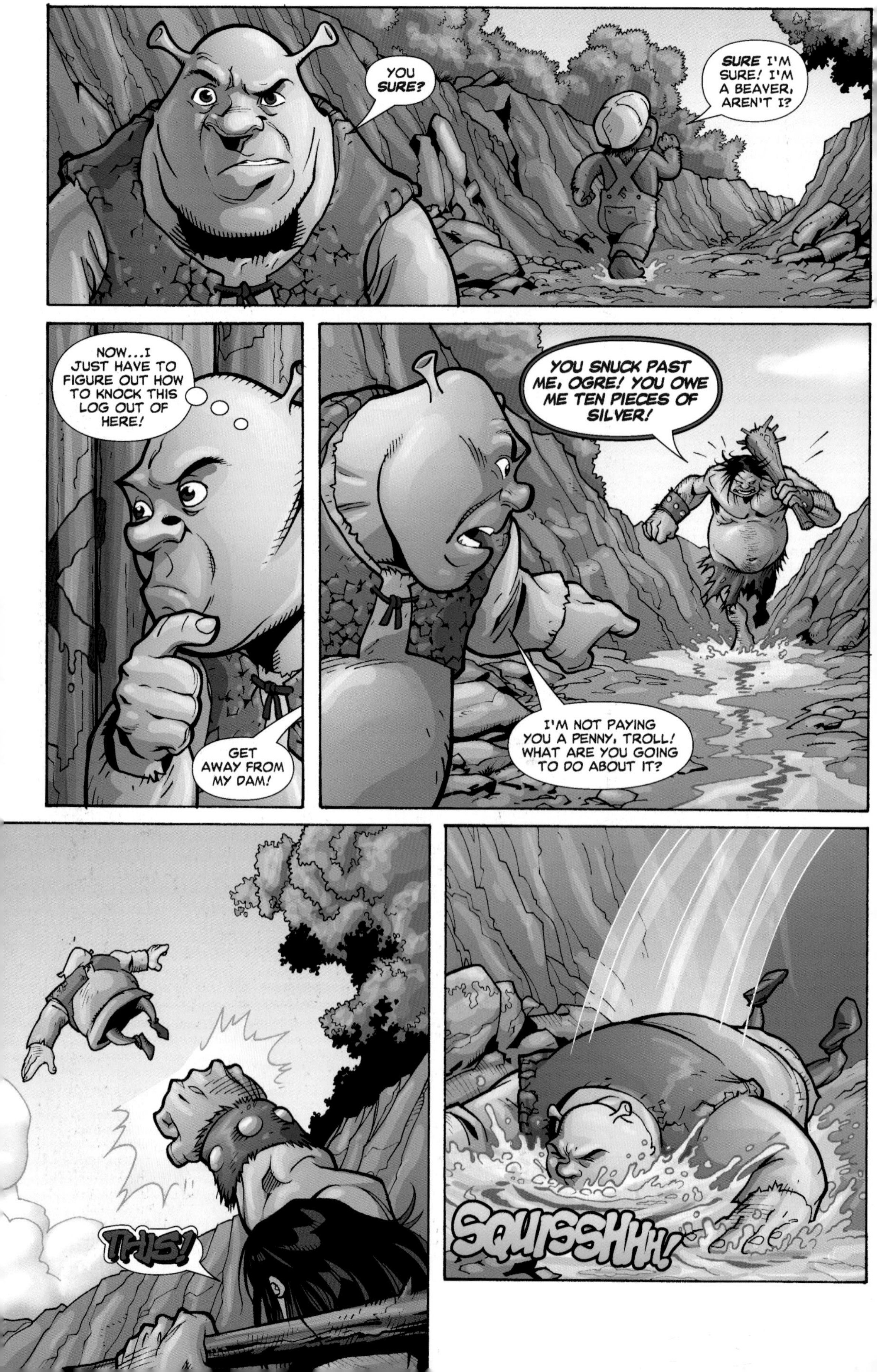
YOU SURE?
SURE I'M SURE! I'M A BEAVER, AREN'T I?
NOW...I JUST HAVE TO FIGURE OUT HOW TO KNOCK THIS LOG OUT OF HERE!
GET AWAY FROM MY DAM!
YOU SNUCK PAST ME, OGRE! YOU OWE ME TEN PIECES OF SILVER!
I'M NOT PAYING YOU A PENNY, TROLL! WHAT ARE YOU GOING TO DO ABOUT IT?
THIS!
SQUISSHHH!

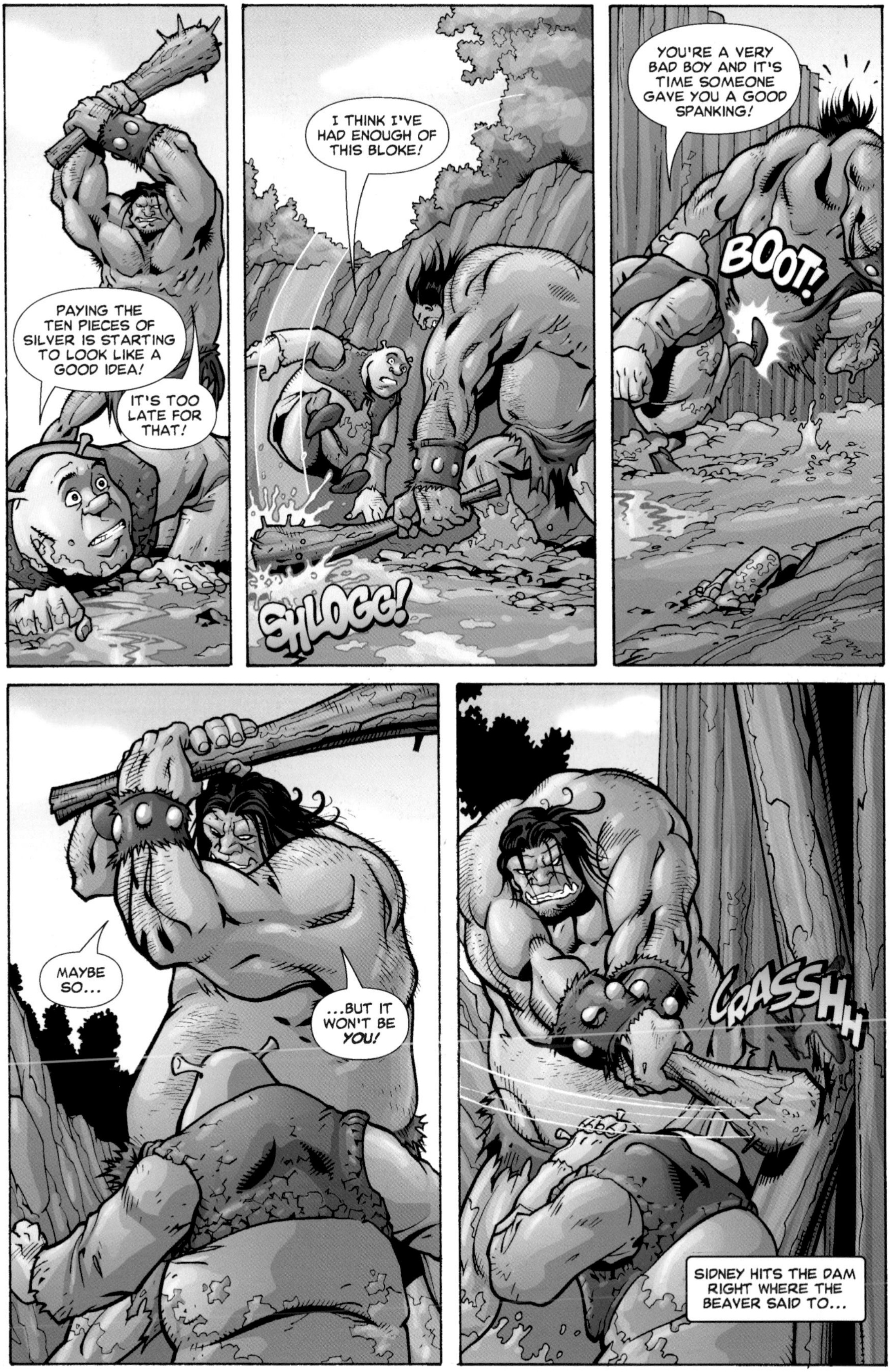
PAYING THE TEN PIECES OF SILVER IS STARTING TO LOOK LIKE A GOOD IDEA!
IT'S TOO LATE FOR THAT!
I THINK I'VE HAD ENOUGH OF THIS BLOKE!
SHLOGG!
YOU'RE A VERY BAD BOY AND IT'S TIME SOMEONE GAVE YOU A GOOD SPANKING!
BOOT!
MAYBE SO...
...BUT IT WON'T BE *YOU!*
CRASSHH
SIDNEY HITS THE DAM RIGHT WHERE THE BEAVER SAID TO...

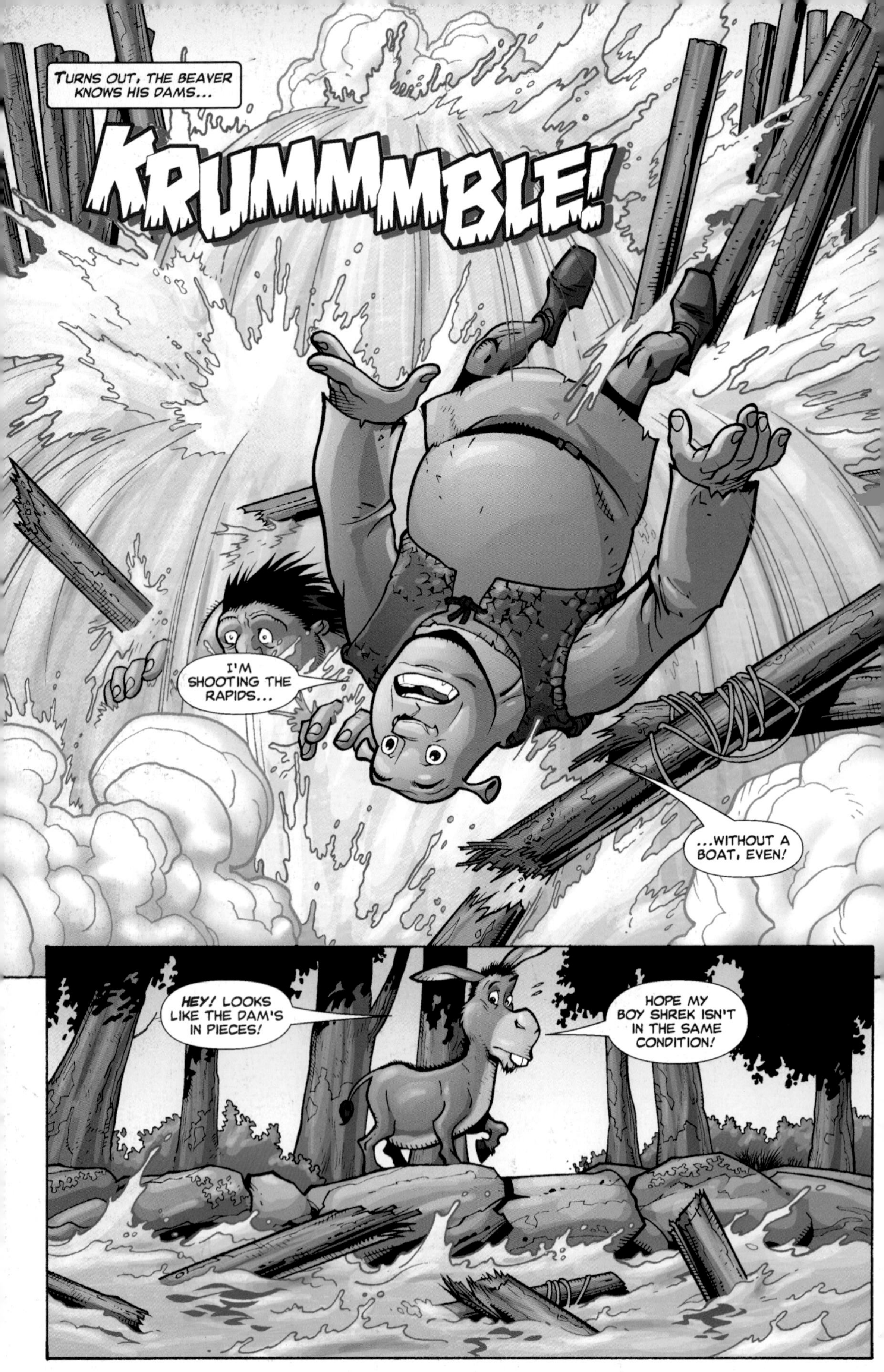
TURNS OUT, THE BEAVER KNOWS HIS DAMS...
KRUMMMMBLE!
I'M SHOOTING THE RAPIDS...
...WITHOUT A BOAT, EVEN!
HEY! LOOKS LIKE THE DAM'S IN PIECES!
HOPE MY BOY SHREK ISN'T IN THE SAME CONDITION!

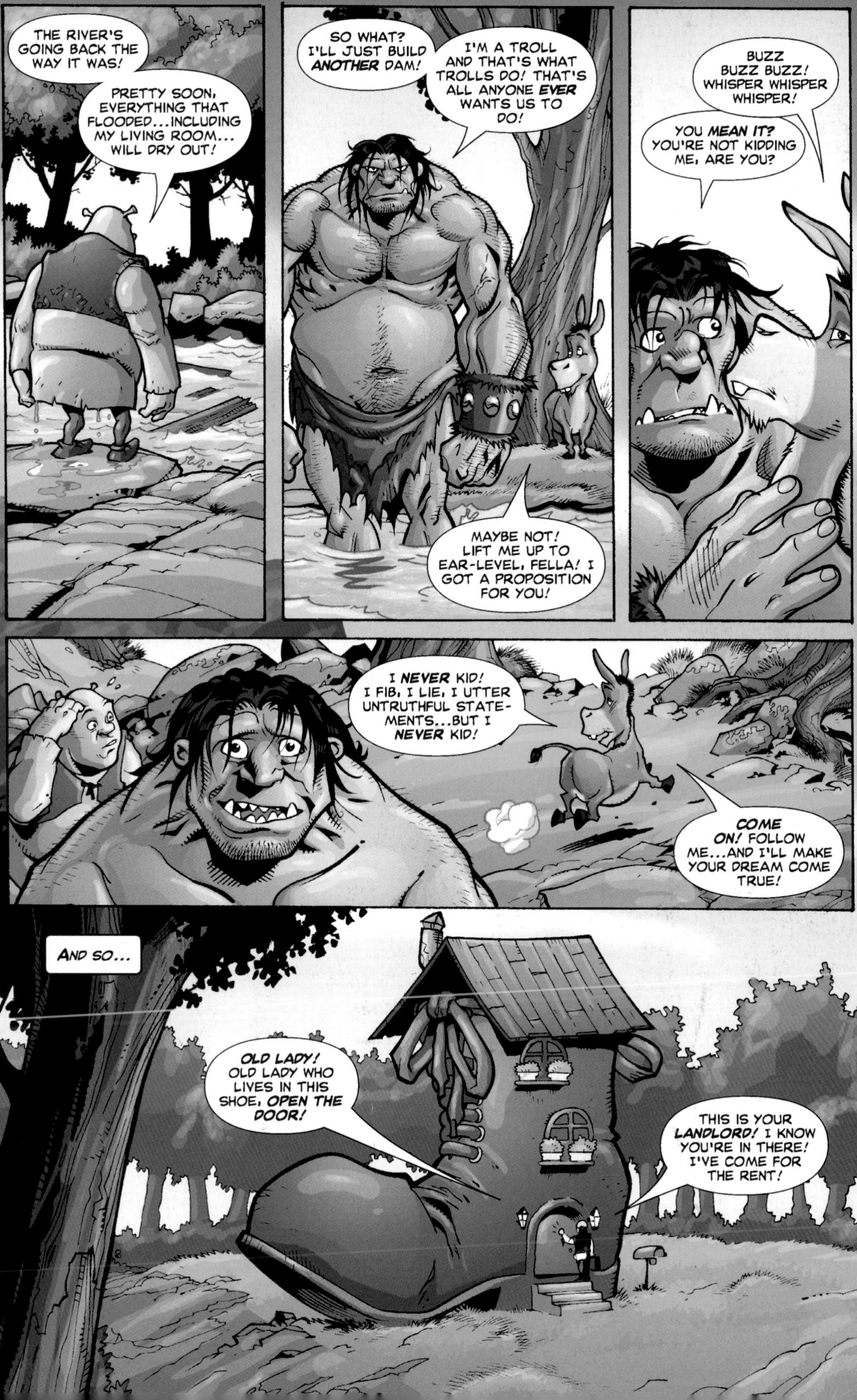
THE RIVER'S GOING BACK THE WAY IT WAS!
PRETTY SOON, EVERYTHING THAT FLOODED...INCLUDING MY LIVING ROOM... WILL DRY OUT!
SO WHAT? I'LL JUST BUILD ANOTHER DAM!
I'M A TROLL AND THAT'S WHAT TROLLS DO! THAT'S ALL ANYONE EVER WANTS US TO DO!
MAYBE NOT! LIFT ME UP TO EAR-LEVEL, FELLA! I GOT A PROPOSITION FOR YOU!
BUZZ BUZZ BUZZ! WHISPER WHISPER WHISPER!
YOU MEAN IT? YOU'RE NOT KIDDING ME, ARE YOU?
I NEVER KID! I FIB, I LIE, I UTTER UNTRUTHFUL STATE-MENTS...BUT I NEVER KID!
COME ON! FOLLOW ME...AND I'LL MAKE YOUR DREAM COME TRUE!
AND SO...
OLD LADY! OLD LADY WHO LIVES IN THIS SHOE, OPEN THE DOOR!
THIS IS YOUR LANDLORD! I KNOW YOU'RE IN THERE! I'VE COME FOR THE RENT!

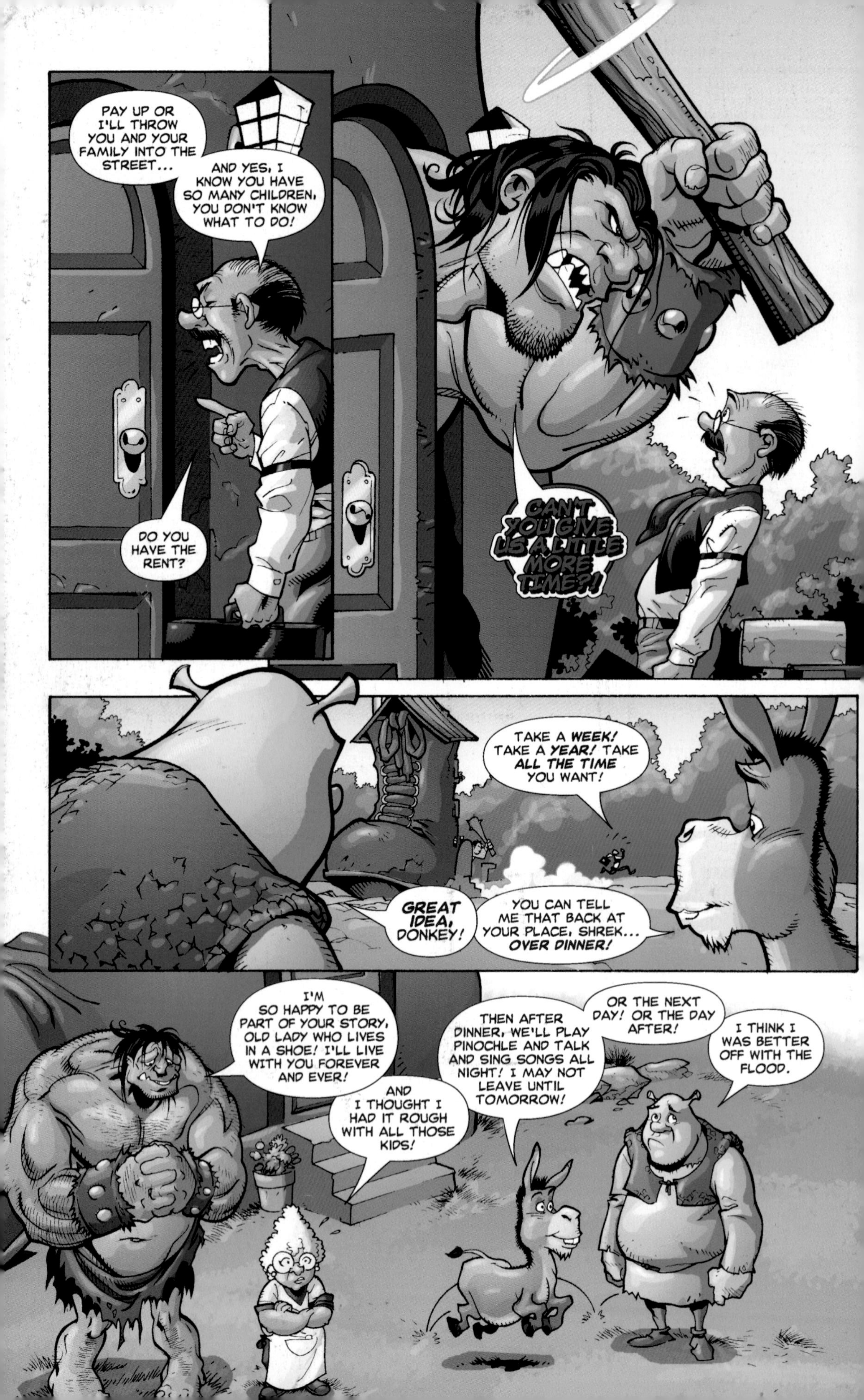
DO YOU HAVE THE RENT?
PAY UP OR I'LL THROW YOU AND YOUR FAMILY INTO THE STREET...
AND YES, I KNOW YOU HAVE SO MANY CHILDREN, YOU DON'T KNOW WHAT TO DO!
CAN'T YOU GIVE US A LITTLE MORE TIME?!
TAKE A WEEK! TAKE A YEAR! TAKE ALL THE TIME YOU WANT!
GREAT IDEA, DONKEY!
YOU CAN TELL ME THAT BACK AT YOUR PLACE, SHREK... OVER DINNER!
I'M SO HAPPY TO BE PART OF YOUR STORY, OLD LADY WHO LIVES IN A SHOE! I'LL LIVE WITH YOU FOREVER AND EVER!
AND I THOUGHT I HAD IT ROUGH WITH ALL THOSE KIDS!
THEN AFTER DINNER, WE'LL PLAY PINOCHLE AND TALK AND SING SONGS ALL NIGHT! I MAY NOT LEAVE UNTIL TOMORROW!
OR THE NEXT DAY! OR THE DAY AFTER!
I THINK I WAS BETTER OFF WITH THE FLOOD.

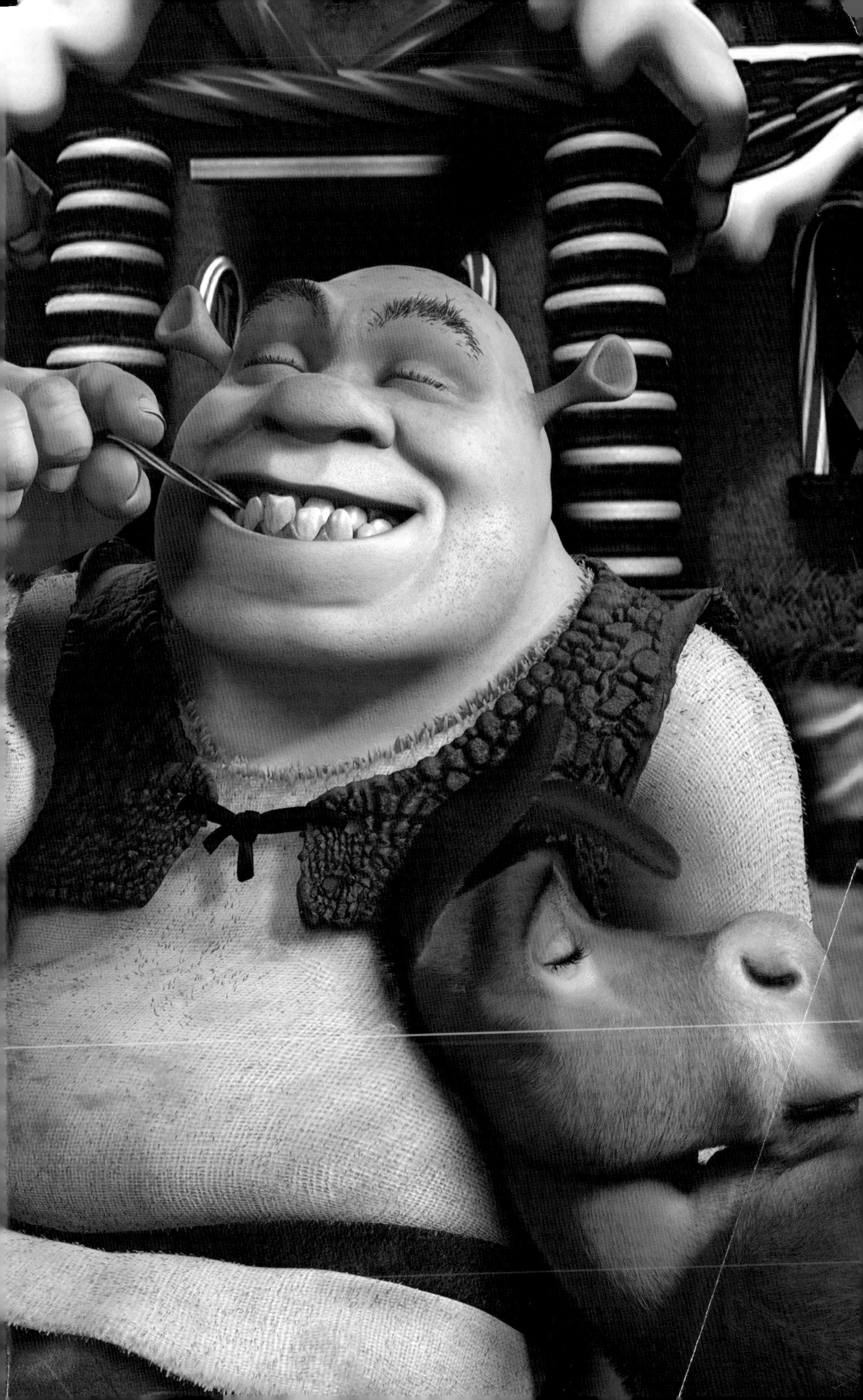

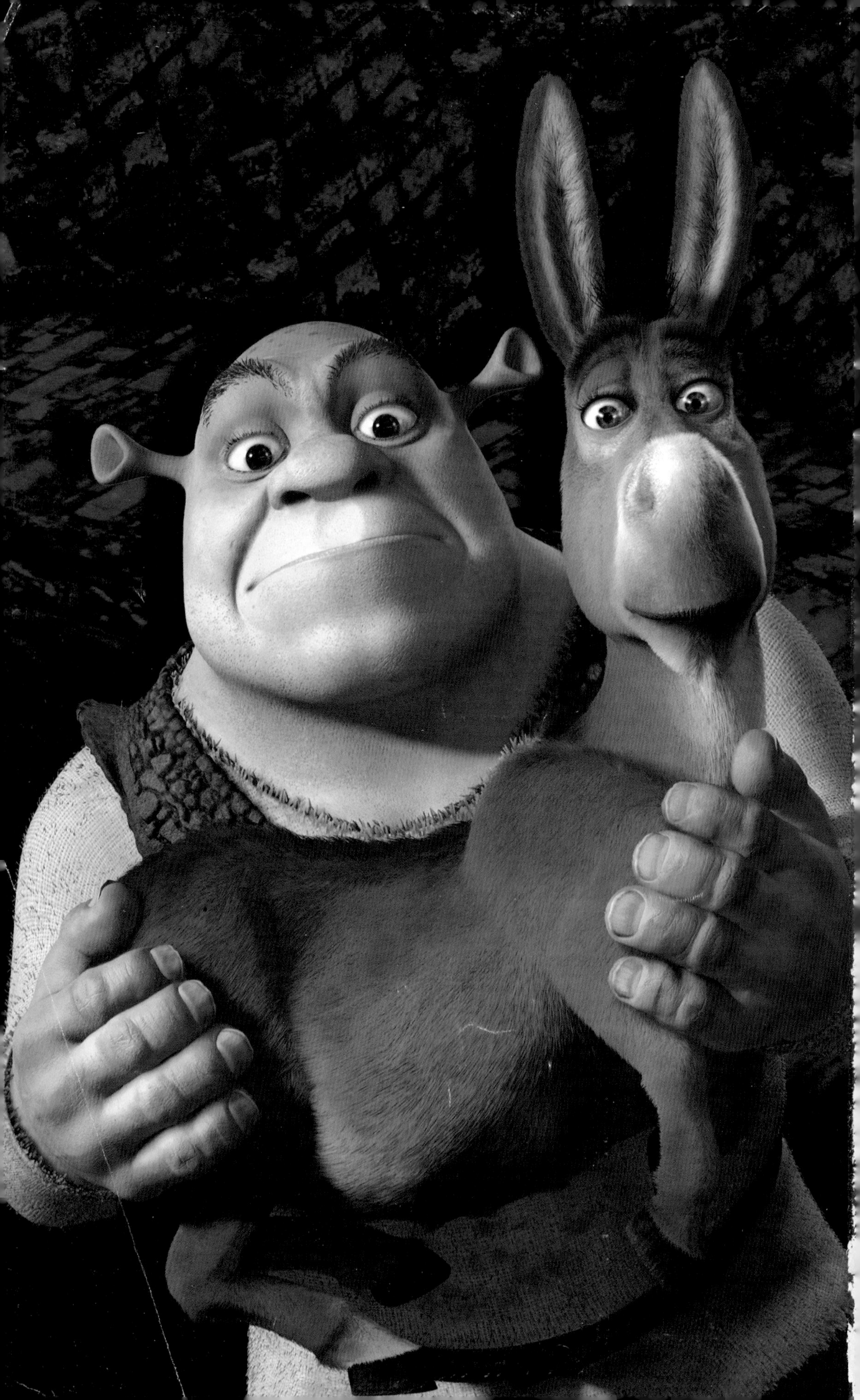